THE SOHO CHARCUTERIE C·O·O·K·B·O·O·K

❦ THE SOHO ❦ CHARCUTERIE C·O·O·K·B·O·O·K

Fabulous Food for Entertaining

by Francine Scherer & Madeline Poley
with a Note on Choosing Wine by Alexis Bespaloff

William Morrow and Company, Inc.   New York

to dave and aida
harry and etta

This book would not exist
but for the tireless cooperation, commitment, and dedication
of Anne Wright.
She has our deepest respect
and appreciation.

ACKNOWLEDGMENTS

To Narcisse Chamberlain, our editor, who went far beyond the call of duty to the call of mercy.

To Bruce Cliborne, who helped to create the salad, soup, main course, and party planning chapters and whose aesthetic sensibility and talent for collaboration increased the joy of this labor.

To Earle Sieveling, whose creative talent may be found in the majority of recipes in the soup chapter.

To Laura Bergman and Jane Stacey, without whom the dessert chapter would be very slim indeed.

To Dale Henderson, who willingly dipped into her vast well of knowledge and esoterica whenever we needed help.

To Mark Hellerman and Sara Foster, who worked on recipes; and to our night staff, who enthusiastically tasted and critiqued our experiments.

SPECIAL THANKS TO AUDREY DAIUTA, WHO TESTED THE BOOK,
and to Judy Knipe for her help with the editing.

And our grateful appreciation also to the past and present staff of the Soho Charcuterie, whose individual talents and creativity have contributed greatly to our success.

FRANCINE SCHERER
MADELINE POLEY

CONTENTS

*I*n the summer of 1974, we opened a small retail food shop on the Lower West Side of New York City and named it the "Chelsea Charcuterie." The most common question asked us was "What is a *charcuterie?*" (generally mispronounced by the neighbors as "chuckerie"). We had both spent enough time in France to become enamored of the French *charcuteries,* "pork stores," with their sumptuous displays of hams, sausages, *pâtés,* and salads. At that time, New York did not offer a middle zone between the many neighborhood delis with their rubber-stamp coleslaw, potato salad, and boiled ham and the fancy gourmet shops stocked with expensive imported canned white asparagus and *foie gras.* We felt inspired by the gulf.

That summer when we opened the Chelsea Charcuterie, we filled our second-hand display refrigerator with fresh *pâtés,* imaginative homemade salads, quiches, German hams, and unusual European cheeses. Our aim was not to imitate the French version but to Americanize it by lifting the New York deli up several palatable notches. We mixed our chicken salad with fresh tarragon; curried mayonnaise, apples, and almonds were blended with tuna. We shopped each day in the local vegetable markets and were inspired by the ingredients available: We made fresh broccoli with garlic and anchovy mayonnaise, green beans with fresh oregano, tomatoes, pepperoni, and riccota cheese. We abandoned quiche Lorraine for quiches made with spinach, bacon, and mushroom, chicken and asparagus, or smoked salmon and shrimp. The lunch trade wanted sandwiches, so we shopped the Lower East Side for crusty black Russian breads and the Upper East Side for croissants, brioches, and French bread. We offered a new breed of sandwiches: brioche stuffed with chicken with tarragon mayonnaise, Black Forest ham and Brie on crusty French loaves, and tuna curry salad on black bread.

Fortunately, the neighborhood responded enthusiastically. (The actor Tony Perkins, who lived in Chelsea, biked to the store each Sunday for a bag of assorted bagels and all the green bean salad we could spare.) After a write-up on *New York* magazine's "Best Bets" page, people from other parts of the city began to seek us out.

Our store was charming (exposed brick walls, fireplace, French windows), but too small to house a kitchen. All our cooking had to take place in our respective apartments, as well as infiltrate the kitchens of sympathetic friends.

One day, in our hurry to drop off a bag of vegetables at a friend's apartment (she had graciously volunteered to blanch them for us), we mistakenly included a paper bag containing money from our weekend business. She called to thank us for our generosity, but said she felt she was being overpaid for a few hours of her time.

It was also disconcerting to have your home kitchen invaded each night by someone hired to bake quiche or roast chicken until dawn. After long hours in the store, there was no haven to crawl home to. Frustration is either the mother of invention or the cause of a nervous breakdown. Being by nature optimistic, we decided to scour the area for a location that would provide us with a most needed kitchen. We looked around Chelsea but didn't find anything suitable. Our real estate search took us farther south to Greenwich Village (too expensive) and finally into the artist district of Soho. Soho renewal was in its early stages, and large spaces were still for rent at reasonable prices. After a few months of looking, we settled on an old vacated Italian restaurant at the corner of Spring and Sullivan streets. It was an abandoned mess, but spacious. Originally, our idea was to do an expanded version of the Chelsea Charcuterie for prepared take-out foods, but the space itself altered our concept. If we built the retail store in the front, there would still be enough room left over to put tables and chairs in the back for a restaurant.

Faced with the possibility of both a restaurant and retail store, we set out to design a space that would reflect the newness of this idea. Soho was becoming known for originality in the conversion of large, open factory lofts into light and airy living spaces where artists could both work and live. Up until that time, the style in restaurants was closed-in and low lighted. Customers would walk off the street from the brightness of day into the dark interior wombs of restaurants. We wanted to have a place that would be light and clean, where people, flowers, and food would create the colors in the environment. We hired Lance Brown, an architect friend of ours, to achieve this end with an unfortunately small budget. The results were satisfying: an all white restaurant with cooling ceiling fans, highly polished light wood floors, and an expanse of small-paned windows to bring in the day. And best of all was the kitchen. Perhaps primitive by some standards, to us it was a luxurious workspace in which to create and not have to live.

We hired a small kitchen staff of people open to new ideas and not wedded to the old traditions. The lunch menu evolved around the colorful selection of salads, which customers passed in the retail store on their way to the restaurant. We added omelets filled with smoked salmon, with sour cream and chives, and with Black Forest ham and Brie, fresh herbs, shallots, and watercress. Quiche fillings changed each day. Salad platters with chicken with tarragon mayonnaise or tuna curry salad or whole jumbo shrimp in herb mayonnaise were garnished lavishly with flowerlike vegetables and were later described by one food writer as aerial views of Tahiti. A Charcuterie sampling of five house salads was provided for avid nibblers. As much effort was put into the presentation of food as its preparation, for we believed that the salivating process should begin the moment the plate was put down in front of the customer.

Although we were ready for Soho and New York, it appeared the reverse was not true. Soho was still "undiscovered," and only an adventuresome few wandered south of Houston Street. (By the way, in New York, the name Soho is an abbreviation of South of Houston.) The local artists and Italian neighbors were supportive in their rank and file—a continuous stream came through the door, expressing congratulations for this new breed of restaurant—but unfortunately they could not afford any financial support. Six months later, we and a dedicated but thinning staff were about to call it quits. I remember how demoralized we were one January evening when two waiters, a busboy, dishwasher, and ourselves sat at a corner table watching our only customer that night eat his dinner. Then three very opportune and supportive reviews appeared in *The New York Times*, *Women's Wear Daily*, and *The Village Voice*. Business soared from our one lonely customer to standing room only. Before long, we were discovered by the celebrities, and tables were reserved by the likes of Geoffrey Beene, Woody Allen, Warren Beatty, and Gilda Radner.

During the early part of our first year, we decided to offer a Sunday brunch menu. It was a favorite meal for both of us, and we wanted to elevate Brunch to its rightful heights—casual, diverse, ethnic, and elegant. Although weekend brunch menus already existed at various New York restaurants, the choices were conventional and did not reflect the ethnic variety of the city; they ranged from uninspired egg dishes and hamburgers with pitchers of Bloody Marys at neighborhood restaurants to the pretentious and expensive offerings of large hotel dining rooms.

When we were children growing up in New York, our parents used to travel on Sunday mornings to the Lower East Side to shop at the row of Jewish food stores on Houston and Orchard streets. Hasidic Jews sold, and still do, pounds of freshly made cream cheeses of a dozen varieties—scallion, strawberry, herb, and raisin and walnut. Next door would be a staggering display of smoked salmon, herrings, sturgeon, whitefish, dried fruits, and vats of pickles and olives. At the bakery were onion breads, bagels, bialies, thick black pumpernickel, and challah. We have continued this pilgrimage into our adult years. But the Jewish food stores are just a small pocket of New York. There are still the German, Polish, French, Irish, Italian sections—so many other ethnic flavors to discover! Why not be inspired by them all to create a truly eclectic brunch menu? We discovered Sonia, barely five feet high, a stocky Polish woman from Second Avenue who daily baked loaves and loaves of the best challah we had ever eaten in a kitchen only three times as wide as herself. The brunch menu began. We transformed her ethereal challah into French toast and served it with Vermont Grade A maple syrup. A few years later *The New York Times* described it as the best French toast in New York and published a cartoon in honor of it.

French Toast

4 servings

2   loaves challah *or* brioche bread

6   extra-large fertilized eggs, at room temperature

2   tablespoons brandy *(optional)*

⅓   cup heavy cream

¼   teaspoon freshly grated nutmeg

2   tablespoons good-quality maple syrup

3   tablespoons freshly squeezed orange juice

¼   teaspoon grated cinnamon stick

1   cup Clarified Butter (page 24)

*U*sing a serated knife, trim the ends of the challah loaves (approximately ¼ inch off each end), then turn the loaf upside down to facilitate measurement and cutting. Slice the loaves into slices 1½ inches thick. (Reserve excess Challah to use for bread crumbs. They are excellent in the Boudin Blanc recipe that appears in this book.) Spread out the challah slices so they can dry slightly.

In a large mixing bowl, mix together thoroughly all the remaining ingredients, except the clarified butter. Tilt the bowl as you stir to insure a smooth mixture. (It must be stirred again immediately before each use, otherwise the egg whites will settle to the bottom and the cinnamon will float to the top.) On a medium-high flame, heat ½ cup of the clarified butter in a frying pan until small bubbles form around the edge.

Place a slice of challah in the batter, pressing down on it gently. Turn it over and repeat on the other side. Lightly squeeze the soaked bread to eliminate excess batter, place it in the heated butter, and cook for 1½ minutes, or until golden brown. With a spatula, chip away any excess batter that seeps out of the bread. Lower the flame, gently slide the spatula under the slice, turn it over, using a cooking fork to guide it, then cook the other side for 30 seconds, or until it is golden brown.

Remove the pan from the burner to prevent butter from overheating while dipping new slices of challah. Before frying the remaining slices, be sure to remove from the butter any small bits of batter or darkened particles of bread. Place all the cooked slices on a baking sheet and place in a preheated 450°F oven for approximately 10 minutes.

NOTE: After frying 4 pieces of French toast it will be necessary to add ¼ cup more clarified butter to the pan.

Serve with flavored butter and syrup, such as orange butter and maple-cinnamon syrup, and garnish with thin slices of orange.

The brunch menu expanded. We made omelets filled with ricotta and mozzarella cheese and fresh tomatoes and with asparagus, ham, and Mornay sauce; an Irish breakfast with soda bread, eggs, ham, Irish bacon, blood sausage, and potatoes; quiche, croissants, smoked fish and herring platters, and special slowly whisked scrambled eggs with mushrooms. Channel 7 News considered our eggs Benedict with German-style ham worthy of a tribute on their show. And we received the highest compliment from the British Broadcasting Company, which did a show on the American phenomenon of Sunday brunch and said we had the best brunch the United States had to offer!

Although we received early acclaim on our lunch and brunch menus, we had yet to equal this acclaim at dinner. The food was good and well reviewed, but we felt dissatisfied. Our early dinner menus were influenced by years of reading traditional French masters such as Escoffier, Henri Pellaprat, Raymond Oliver, or the American authorities, Julia Child and James Beard. Excellent teachers, but where was our identity? It wasn't until we spent an August vacation in France dining at the three-star restaurants of Roger Vergé, Alain Chapel, Michel Guérard, and the Troisgros brothers that our own style started to emerge. What we experienced at the tables of these great chefs was exhilarating. Their inspiration began with the freshness of local ingredients, and delicate sauces became the complementary backdrop to food. An observation of Oriental cuisine enhanced the flavor and texture of vegetables and fish. Each dish was exquisitely plated and presented. After all, some of these principles we had applied to our other menus; why were we so cowardly as not to take the same creative risks after six o'clock?

Back again in New York, we abandoned cans of tasteless truffles and *morilles* (superb in France because they were fresh) and began our search for the best local ingredients. A retired woman from Pennsylvania brought us a luxurious variety of garden fresh herbs. A two-hour drive to a dairy farm in New Jersey rewarded us with glass bottles filled with thick yellow cream. (Some of it even turned to butter on the bumpy drive back.) We found fresh Muscovy ducks and scallops with the roe still attached. In the summer, we battled the vacation traffic to the Hamptons on Long Island for vegetables from a farm in Watermill that grew exotic golden beets, purple string beans, chocolate-colored peppers, and low-acid yellow tomatoes.

We began to study regional American cooking. For a long time restaurants had generally imitated the cooking of other countries—Greek, French, Italian, Chinese. What was sorely missing was the American creative process, the ability and talent to integrate into one's own style the influences of both fine regional and international cooking. Our experience in France indicated that our inspiration must take root in the availability of local products. Local Long Island duck and homemade spicy Acadian sausages with gumbo sauce began to appear on our menu. Recently Mimi Sheraton, restaurant critic for *The New York Times*, summarized our new attitude toward dinner when she named the Soho Charcuterie as part of the ". . . emerging American cuisine."

Over the years, we have been approached by enthusiastic customers to open replicas of the Soho Charcuterie in other cities. Although we were tempted (and almost got as far as scouting out a location in Beverly Hills), we knew that our restaurant had worked because of our daily effort and concern, on the spot, and a talented staff. Fine food must be lovingly prepared with a constant eye on freshness, flavor, and everything that happens in the kitchen.

We hope our readers will enjoy re-creating the recipes offered in this book. Both the Soho Charcuterie and an active catering business have taught us how many people today care about good cooking and search for ideas for entertaining at home. They come to us most often for elegant food for parties in the informal American style—buffets, suppers, festive picnics and outdoor parties, as well as brunch on Sunday. Therefore, out of the several hundred recipes we and our staff have created in the past nine years, we've selected chiefly those that work well for such parties. We hope you will agree that an omelet, salad, or sandwich can and should be a noble offering. We've used recipes that can be made quickly and others that are more challenging, a full range. Quite ambitious are our recipes for charcuterie fare, which could well make your reputation as a cook; one of their virtues is that they *must* be done well ahead. A majority of the recipes in the book can, in fact, be made ahead, which is important for party menus—and we give their life-spans, that is, how far ahead they can be made and still be served at their best. To round out the book, in the Main Courses chapter we have included some of our favorites from our dinner menu so that you will have more dishes to choose from for dinner parties. And at the end, Alexis Bespaloff has contributed a fine chapter on the art of choosing wines, which we've followed by a chapter on party and menu planning and recipes for cocktail hors d'oeuvre. So we think we've touched all the bases for fabulous food for your parties.

FRANCINE SCHERER
MADELINE POLEY

Eggs

*T*he versatile egg is the base for five distinct types of recipes in this chapter—eggs poached, eggs scrambled, cold hard-cooked eggs, omelets, and soufflés.

All eggs are extra-large (and fertilized, if possible).

In all egg preparations, when butter is called for, it should be sweet (unsalted) butter. Clarified butter (page 24) is not usually specified, but it is excellent for omelets and is also used elsewhere in this book.

POACHED EGGS

To Poach Eggs

8   **extra-large eggs**

1   **tablespoon white vinegar**

1   **teaspoon kosher** *or* **sea salt**

    Bowl of cold water for cooked eggs

*F*ill a large stainless-steel skillet (10- to 12-inch minimum) two thirds full of water. Add the vinegar (to hasten the coagulation of the egg white) and the salt (to help the vinegar achieve its role). Bring the water to a boil and lower to a simmer. There should be a steady movement of small bubbles from the bottom of the pan, but nothing approaching a "roll."

Break each egg into a cup and slide them one by one (see NOTE) gently into the center of the simmer. The heat and movement of the water must be maintained at a level that provides a bit of buoyancy for the egg without actually violently boiling around it, which would cook it too quickly and disrupt the shaping. Count 6–8 seconds (at that point the egg will begin to rise) and then, with a wooden spoon, gently lift one side of the forming egg white over the yolk, making certain that it reaches to the opposite side, where it will attach as it cooks, encasing the yolk. Cook 1 minute and then gently slide a slotted spoon under the egg and roll it over.

The eggs are cooked when the whites become opaque but the yolks are still liquid, approximately 1 minute on each side. Remove to the bowl of cold water with the slotted spoon; this halts the cooking. Set poaching water aside but do not discard. Trim off excess raggedy egg whites with the spoon and set aside the bowl of eggs.

At this point follow the instructions for the preparation of the poached egg recipe you are using. When you are ready to serve the eggs, put them back into the simmering poaching water for 30 seconds in order *just* to reheat them. Gently lift out each egg with the slotted spoon, allowing the water to drain off completely.

NOTE: Don't try to poach more than 4 eggs at a time, as the loss of heat in the water will be too great. Also, it is difficult to control the cooking of more than 4 eggs at once.

Eggs Benedict

*P*repare the components for eggs Benedict in the order given. Only the English muffins need to be done at the last minute; the other elements can be kept warm or gently reheated just before the dish is assembled.

8   warm Poached Eggs (see *preceding recipe*)

2   cups hollandaise sauce

1   pound Madeira-flavored Black Forest ham

4   English muffins

Hollandaise Sauce

4   extra-large egg yolks

1½   tablespoons freshly squeezed lemon juice

2   tablespoons warm water

¾   teaspoon salt

2–3   grinds pepper

A pinch of cayenne pepper

¾   pound (3 sticks) sweet butter, cut into ½-inch cubes (leave butter at room temperature for 30 minutes)

In a medium-size heavy-bottomed saucepan, combine all the ingredients except the butter. Set over very low heat. With a whisk, beat the mixture until it is thickened and foamy. You must be sure to whisk constantly from the bottom of the pan. This will prevent the mixture from overcooking; the idea is to warm but not cook the yolks.

Still whisking, begin adding the softened butter, 3 or 4 bits at a time, making certain that each addition is thoroughly incorporated before adding the next. Test the temperature of the sauce with your finger from time to time and adjust the heat slightly to keep the sauce warm. When all the butter has been incorporated, beat in up to 1 tablespoon of *warm* water to lighten the sauce. If it is not completely smooth (that is, has bits of cooked egg in it), strain it through a fine-mesh sieve.

Hollandaise can be kept over a pan of hot water, with the water just touching the bottom of the pan, for several hours at room temperature. Cover the surface of the sauce with plastic wrap to prevent a "skin" from forming. If the sauce seems too stiff, beat in up to 1 more tablespoon warm water just before serving.

Madeira-flavored Black Forest Ham

4   tablespoons sweet butter

3   tablespoons Madeira wine

1   pound lean Black Forest ham, cut into 16
     thin slices

In a 10- or 12-inch frying pan, melt the butter over moderate heat and stir in the Madeira. Add the ham slices and heat them for 30 minutes on each side. Cover and set aside in a warm place until ready for final assembly.

Assembly

Split the English muffins in half with a fork. Toast them until lightly browned, butter them or not, as you prefer, and keep them warm.

Meanwhile, warm 4 dinner plates. Place 2 muffin halves on each. Lift the ham slices out of the pan juices, fold or drape 2 slices over each muffin half, and top them with a poached egg. Nap each egg with 3 spoonfuls of the hollandaise sauce and serve promptly.

Suggested garnish: Finely chopped parsley or chives.

Eggs Benedict with Pommes Anna Chips
4 servings

The potatoes in this recipe replace the usual English muffins. They are inspired by a recipe in *Les recettes originales de Jean et Pierre Troisgros, Cuisiniers à Roanne.*

8   warm Poached Eggs (page 20)

8   Pommes Anna Chips

2   cups Hollandaise Sauce (see *preceding recipe*)

1   pound or 16 slices Madeira-flavored Black Forest ham (see *preceding recipe*)

Pommes Anna Chips

1½–1¾   pounds Idaho potatoes

½   teaspoon salt

¼   teaspoon freshly ground pepper

¾   cup warm Clarified Butter (see *following recipe*)

Peel the potatoes and cut them into very thin slices (as for potato chips), using a vegetable peeler, a *mandoline*, or a slicing machine. Drop the slices as they are cut into a bowl of ice water to keep them from discoloring. The slices need not be regularly shaped, but it is important that they be of equal thinness. (This shaving process is fussy but well worth the effort.)

Preheat the oven to 425°F.

Drain the potatoes, dry them thoroughly by pressing them between dish towels, and put them in a medium-size bowl. Add the salt, pepper, and clarified butter and mix together well. Divide the mixture into 8 equal portions. In a large shallow roasting pan or on a jelly-roll pan, form 8 individual pommes Anna chips: Overlap the slices of potato into 8 tight circles measuring approximately 3 inches in diameter, patting and molding them into shape. Place the chips in the oven for 10–15 minutes, or until the edges start to turn a light brown color. You may now take the potatoes from the oven and set them aside.

Just before serving, bake the chips for an additional 10–15 minutes, or until they reach a uniformly golden-brown color. Check them often to make certain they do not burn. Lift the chips gently off the pan with a spatula and transfer them to 4 warmed plates, ready for final assembly.

NOTE: Pommes Anna chips can be kept warm for 1–2 hours after they are browned. Or they may be tightly wrapped and refrigerated overnight and reheated quickly at 450°–500°F. for 3–5 minutes.

Assembly

Place 2 thin slices of Black Forest ham on each of the potato circles. On the ham place 2 poached eggs, nap each egg with 3 spoonfuls of the hollandaise sauce, and serve promptly.

Clarified Butter

*P*ut the desired quantity of sweet butter in a heavy-bottomed saucepan, place over very low heat, and let it melt slowly until the particles of sediment (curd and whey) sink to the bottom of the pan and the foam stops rising to the surface. With a spoon, skim off the foam, diligently removing every particle. Remove from the heat and when the butter reaches room temperature cover the pan with a lid or aluminum foil. Refrigerate overnight. When the butter has solidified, with a spoon very carefully scoop the yellow clarified butter out of the pan and discard the milky liquid sediment in the bottom. Store in a covered container in the refrigerator.

Half a pound of butter will take approximately 15–20 minutes to clarify; a larger quantity can take as long as 1 hour.

Poached Eggs with Sliced Eggplant and Tomato Sauce
4 servings

8	warm Poached Eggs (page 20)
8	slices peeled eggplant, ¼–½ inch thick
	Salt
½	cup all-purpose flour
2	extra-large eggs, beaten
¾	cup bread crumbs
½	pound (2 sticks) sweet butter *or* ¾ cup olive oil
1	cup Tomato Sauce (see *following recipe*)
3	tablespoons chopped fresh herbs *(optional)*

*S*prinkle the eggplant slices with salt and allow to drain on paper towels for 30 minutes. Pat dry. Dredge the slices in the flour, dip into the eggs, and coat with the bread crumbs, pressing them on. Refrigerate for 30 minutes. Melt the butter or heat the oil in a large frying pan over moderate heat, add the eggplant slices, and cook until golden on both sides. Drain the eggplant on paper towels and keep warm until ready for final assembly.

Assembly

Heat the tomato sauce; have ready 4 warm dinner plates. In the center of each plate, place 2 slices of eggplant, top each with a poached egg, nap the eggs with ¼ cup of sauce, and sprinkle with the herbs. Serve promptly.

Tomato Sauce
Makes 4 cups

6	cups purée of fresh tomatoes (approximately 5 pounds tomatoes) *or* canned plum tomatoes (see NOTE)
¼	cup minced shallots (5 large shallots)
2	cloves garlic, minced
½	cup fruity olive oil
¼	cup chopped Italian or regular parsley
¼	cup chopped fresh basil *(optional)*
1½	teaspoons salt
1⅓	cups dry white wine or vermouth
½	teaspoon freshly ground black pepper
	Food mill with medium blade or food processor

*C*oarsely chop seeded tomatoes by hand and pass them through the food mill. Or cut in chunks and purée in the food processor.

In a 10-inch skillet, over a medium flame, sauté the shallots and garlic in the oil without browning them, until they are translucent. Add the tomatoes, parsley, basil, and salt and cook for 3 minutes. Add the wine and cook for approximately 30 minutes, or until the sauce is thick. Add the pepper after the sauce is finished. This sauce freezes well.

NOTE: If using canned tomatoes, drain off the liquid, then pass the tomatoes through the food mill.

Poached Eggs with Vegetable Purée and Beurre Blanc

4 servings

8   warm Poached Eggs (page 20)

Celery Root and Apple Purée

Beurre Blanc

Celery Root and Apple Purée

1   pound celery root

½   pound apples

1   quart milk

2   teaspoons salt

¼   rounded teaspoon freshly ground pepper

3   tablespoons *Crème Fraîche* (page 27) *or* sour cream

3   tablespoons sweet butter

¼   cup chopped fresh herbs (parsley, dill, chives)

Blender or *food processor*

*P*eel the celery root and cut it into 8 equal pieces. Peel, core, and quarter the apples. Put the celery root in a saucepan, add the milk, salt, and pepper and bring to a boil over high heat. Lower the heat, partially cover the pan, and simmer for 15 minutes. At this point add the apples and simmer for 10 minutes, or until the apples and celery root are fork-tender.

Drain the apples and celery root over a bowl, saving the cooking liquid. Put the apples and celery root in the blender or food processor, add 1 tablespoon of the *crème fraîche*, and blend for a total of 3 minutes, adding the remaining *crème fraîche* and the butter as the mixture is puréeing. To thin the purée, add a small amount of the reserved cooking liquid (no more than ¼ cup) and blend for 1 more minute. Taste for salt and pepper. Add 3 tablespoons of the chopped fresh herbs.

To reheat, place the purée in a small, tightly covered baking dish in a 500°F. oven for 5 minutes.

Beurre Blanc

2   tablespoons finely minced shallots

1   cup Muscadet wine

½   teaspoon salt

¾   pound (3 sticks) sweet butter, cut into ½-inch cubes (leave butter at room temperature for 30 minutes)

⅛   teaspoon freshly ground pepper

Prepare just like *Beurre Rouge* (page 29).

Assembly

In the center of a dinner plate put 2 mounds of the vegetable purée (approximately ⅓ cup per egg). In the center of mound put a poached egg. Nap each egg with 2 spoonfuls of *beurre blanc*. Sprinkle with the remaining fresh herbs and serve promptly.

Crème Fraîche
Makes 2 cups

2   cups heavy cream (preferably not ultra-pasteurized)

2   teaspoons buttermilk

Spot-check thermometer

*I*n the top of a double boiler, over simmering water, combine the cream and the buttermilk and heat slowly until the liquid is lukewarm (85° F.). Pour into a glass jar, cover, and allow to sit in a warm place (75°F., a turned-off oven with pilot light, for example) until the cream has thickened, about 8–18 hours. Store in the refrigerator for up to 2 weeks.

Poached Eggs with Oyster Cream Sauce

4 servings

8   warm Poached Eggs (page 20)

Oyster Cream Sauce

Chopped fresh chives *(optional garnish)*

Oyster Cream Sauce

1   cup dry vermouth

½   teaspoon salt

10   grinds pepper

1½   cups heavy cream

White of 1 small leek, cut into julienne strips

1   medium carrot, cut into julienne strips

16   shucked oysters, plus liquid (or about ½ pound shucked)

*I*n an 8- or 10-inch stainless-steel frying pan, over a medium-low flame, reduce the vermouth by half. Add the salt, pepper, and heavy cream and continue to reduce the mixture until it reaches spoon-coating consistency; this will take approximately 7–10 minutes. Add the leek and carrot and continue to simmer the sauce until the vegetables are tender but still crunchy, approximately 1–2 minutes. Add the oysters and their liquid and poach over an extremely low flame until oyster flaps become "ruffled," about 1 minute. If the sauce has become too thin, remove the oysters and vegetables with a slotted spoon and continue reducing the sauce until spoon-coating consistency is reached. Return the oysters and vegetables to the sauce only after the pan has been removed from heat.

Assembly

Have ready 4 warm dinner plates. Place 2 poached eggs on each. On top of or around the eggs place 4 oysters. Tuck one quarter of the vegetables between the eggs. Nap each egg with 2–3 spoonfuls of sauce and garnish with the chopped chives, if desired. Serve promptly.

Tenderloin of Beef with Poached Eggs and Beurre Rouge
4 servings

*P*repare the component parts of this recipe in the order given. Cook the garnish of mushrooms or ham before you make the sauce, keep warm, but do not allow to overcook.

8   warm Poached Eggs (page 20)

   Beurre Rouge

8   slices beef tenderloin (1½ pounds)

   Optional garnishes:

   Sautéed mushrooms *or* 8 thin slices
   Madeira-flavored Black Forest ham (see
   NOTE)

Beurre Rouge

2   tablespoons finely minced shallots

1   cup Beaujolais wine *or* Muscadet for a
   Beurre Blanc

½   teaspoon salt

¾   pound (3 sticks) sweet butter, cut into
   ½-inch cubes (leave butter at room
   temperature for 30 minutes)

⅛   teaspoon freshly ground pepper

In a medium-size heavy-bottomed saucepan, combine the shallots, wine, and salt, bring to a boil, and reduce over a moderate flame for 10–15 minutes, or until the liquid has nearly disappeared. There should be a soft, juicy but *not liquid* "marmalade" left. Remove the pan from the heat and with a whisk, gradually add a few small chunks of the softened butter, stirring constantly until the butter is smooth and creamy. Reduce the flame to very low and return the pan to the heat. Continue adding the butter, 3 or 4 chunks at a time, whisking constantly until all of it is incorporated. Too much heat will result in an oily, separated mess; not enough heat will cause the sauce to congeal. Therefore, to control the temperature, you must move the pan on and off the burner. Keep checking the temperature of the sauce with your finger to make certain it stays warm—the temperature for baby's milk. ("This sauce is a rich creamy emulsion, not thick, but with a distinct firm body," says Richard Olney in *Simple French Cooking.*) Whisk in the pepper. Set aside in a warm place or in a water bath.

Beef Tenderloin

1½   **pounds trimmed tenderloin of beef**
  4   **tablespoons Clarified Butter (page 24)**
      Freshly ground pepper to taste
      Salt to taste

Slice meat into eight 2½- to 3-ounce portions and pat dry with paper towels; it will not sear properly if it is damp. Lightly pepper both sides of the slices. Coat the surface of a 10-inch frying pan with 2 tablespoons of the butter and heat until very hot but not smoking. Add 4 slices of the beef and sear them quickly on both sides, approximately 30 seconds to a side. With a spatula, remove them to a plate. Pour off any burnt butter, replenish the pan with more butter, and cook the remaining 4 slices. Lightly salt the 8 pieces of meat.

Assembly

Have ready 4 warm dinner plates. Place 2 slices of sautéed beef on each. Top each slice with a poached egg, and nap each egg with 2 spoonfuls of *beurre rouge.* Garnish as desired and serve promptly.

NOTE: **For a sautéed mushroom garnish:** 1 cup thinly sliced fresh *shiitake,* morel, or other wild mushrooms, 2 tablespoons minced shallots, and 1 teaspoon chopped chives briefly sautéed together in 1½ tablespoons sweet butter over moderate heat without browning, for about 5 minutes. Add salt, pepper, and freshly squeezed lemon juice to taste. Place mushrooms on tenderloin slices before adding poached eggs.

For a ham garnish: See Madeira-flavored Black Forest Ham (page 22). Sauté as directed 8 thin slices (½ recipe) Black Forest or other good-quality ham and place on tenderloin slices before adding poached eggs.

Tenderloin of Beef with Poached Eggs and Roquefort Sauce

4 servings

*P*repare as in the preceding recipe, substituting Roquefort sauce for the *beurre rouge*.

8   warm Poached Eggs (page 20)

Roquefort sauce

8   slices beef tenderloin (1½ pounds)

Crisp crumbled bacon mixed with chopped fresh herbs *(optional garnish)*

Roquefort Sauce

1   cup dry vermouth

1   teaspoon finely chopped shallots

1½   cups heavy cream

Salt to taste

1½   ounces Roquefort cheese, crumbled

1   tablespoon very soft sweet butter

10   grinds pepper

In an 8- or 10-inch stainless-steel frying pan, over a medium-low flame, reduce the vermouth and shallots to ½ cup. Add the cream and salt and continue to reduce the mixture. Meanwhile, in a small bowl, with the back of a spoon blend together the cheese and butter. When the cream-and-vermouth mixture has reduced by one third, or reaches a light napping consistency, remove the pan from the heat and whisk in the cheese and butter mixture. Add pepper and salt to taste.

NOTE: You can judge the consistency of the sauce by how it coats the back of a spoon: When it covers the surface of the spoon with a uniform glaze, the desired "napping" stage has been achieved.

SCRAMBLED EGGS

Scrambled Eggs with Fines Herbes

4 servings

10	extra-large eggs, at room temperature
3	tablespoons heavy cream
½	teaspoon salt
¼	teaspoon freshly ground pepper
6	tablespoons sweet butter, in all
2	tablespoons chopped parsley
¼	cup chopped watercress
1	tablespoon chopped fresh chives
1	tablespoon chopped fresh dill
½	cup cottage cheese or ricotta cheese (optional)

*I*n a large mixing bowl, beat together the eggs, cream, salt, and pepper for 1 minute and set aside. In a large frying pan, melt 4 tablespoons of the butter over a low flame, add the herbs, and cook them for 30 seconds in order to release their flavor. At this point, adjust the flame to medium-low and add the egg mixture. Using a metal spoon, stir constantly, making certain to scrape the sides and bottom of the pan repeatedly; this prevents the eggs from sticking and scorching and is also vital for the forming of soft curds. If the scraping process gets out of control, lower the flame. Gradually, in approximately 5 minutes, all the liquid egg is scraped and stirred until the desired consistency is reached and the eggs form soft creamy mounds. Immediately remove the pan from the heat and quickly stir in the remaining 2 tablespoons of butter cut into small pieces. This stops the cooking and preserves the texture of the eggs. At this point, you may stir in the cottage or ricotta cheese, if desired.

NOTE: Scrambled Eggs with *Fines Herbes* may be used as a filling for Spinach Crêpes (page 60).

Scrambled Eggs
with Smoked Salmon and Onions
4 servings

10   extra-large eggs, at room temperature

2   tablespoons heavy cream

¼   pound (1 stick) sweet butter, in all

6   heaping tablespoons chopped onion or 4 tablespoons chopped shallots

6   ounces smoked salmon, coarsely chopped

½   teaspoon freshly ground pepper

1   tablespoon chopped parsley

1   tablespoon chopped fresh chives

   Salt *(optional)*

*I*n a large mixing bowl, beat together the eggs and the cream for 1 minute and set aside. In a large frying pan, melt 6 tablespoons of the butter over a low flame, add the onion, and sauté for 2–4 minutes until it is translucent. Add the salmon and season with pepper, then add the egg mixture and adjust the heat to medium. Scramble the eggs as described in the preceding recipe. Off the heat stir in the remaining 2 tablespoons of butter and the parsley and chives. Add up to ¼ teaspoon salt, depending on the saltiness of the salmon you have used.

NOTE: Scrambled Eggs with Smoked Salmon and Onions may be used as a filling for Spinach Crêpes (page 60).

Eggs Escoffier

3 servings

*I*n classic French cooking, scrambled eggs were allowed only when cooked in a *bain-marie*. Today's double boiler also insures that the eggs will not overcook and that they will be kept soft and creamy. The lengthy procedure in this recipe guarantees the finest of egg preparations.

8	extra-large eggs, at room temperature
½	teaspoon salt
¼	teaspoon freshly ground pepper
4½	tablespoons heavy cream, in all
4	tablespoons sweet butter
1	tablespoon finely minced shallot, firmly packed
¼	cup fresh *shiitake* or other wild mushrooms, finely minced and firmly packed

Double boiler, 1-quart capacity

In a medium-size mixing bowl, with a large fork, blend together the eggs, salt, pepper, and 2 tablespoons of the cream and set aside.

In the top of the double boiler, over water at a high simmer, melt 2 table-spoons of the butter, cut into small pieces. Add the shallot and mushrooms and allow them to soften, about 5 minutes.

Add the egg mixture. Stir constantly with a small whisk. (A fine-wire whisk works much better than a stiffer whisk with fewer wires.) Take, as Es-coffier suggests, "care to avoid cooking too quickly, which, by instantaneously solidifying the egg molecules, would cause lumps to form in the mass—a thing which, above all, should be guarded against." The ultimate objective is an egg mass that is light, fairly smooth, and creamy in texture.

The method is very gradual. Adjust the heat to control the speed of the cooking. After 2 minutes at a high simmer, lower the flame until the water in the double boiler is at a medium simmer, with only a few bubbles breaking the surface of the water. Stir constantly until the eggs form soft peaks, approximately 10–15 minutes. Remove from the heat and whisk in the remaining cream and butter. Serve immediately.

Serving suggestions: Place a hollowed-out warm brioche on its side and fill one third of it with some of the eggs. Pastry shells can also be used as attractive containers for these eggs.

HARD-COOKED EGGS

To Boil Eggs
6–8 eggs

6–8   extra-large eggs

1   teaspoon salt

1   teaspoon vinegar

*P*ut the eggs in a 2-quart saucepan, cover with cold water, add the salt and vinegar, and bring to a boil. Turn off the heat and allow the eggs to sit undisturbed for 20 minutes. Pour off the hot water and quickly submerge the eggs in cold water for 2–3 minutes, or until you can handle them easily.

Provençal Stuffed Eggs

4 servings

6   Hard-Cooked Eggs (see *preceding recipe*),
    halved lengthwise

Ratatouille

⅓   cup olive oil

1   heaping cup diced yellow squash or zucchini

1   heaping cup diced red or green bell peppers

1   heaping cup peeled and diced eggplant

¼   cup finely chopped onion

2   small cloves garlic, minced

1   cup Tomato Sauce (page 25)

1   teaspoon salt

½   teaspoon freshly ground pepper

¼   cup chopped fresh herbs *(optional)*

*I*n a 10- to 12-inch skillet, over a medium flame, heat the
olive oil, add all the ingredients, except the tomato sauce, salt, pepper, and
herbs, and sauté without browning until the vegetables are tender, approximately 5 minutes. Stir in the tomato sauce, salt, pepper, and herbs and transfer
the *ratatouille* to a bowl. Set aside.

Egg-Yolk Stuffing

The 6 hard-cooked egg yolks

1½   tablespoons purée of olives or 10 black
     olives cured in oil, pitted, peeled, and
     minced

¼   teaspoon freshly ground pepper

2   tablespoons olive oil

1½   tablespoons sweet butter, at room
     temperature

½ teaspoon salt (omit if you use anchovies)

4 salted anchovy fillets, finely chopped
(optional)

Chopped scallion

In a small bowl, mash all the ingredients together with a fork until they are well combined. Stuff the egg-white halves by spreading one twelfth of the mixture evenly over the entire cut side of each one. Set aside.

Assembly

Heat the tomato sauce. Put ¼ cup of it in the middle of 4 dinner plates. On each plate place 2 egg halves, stuffing side down and 2 inches apart, in the center of the sauce. Place about ½ cup *ratatouille* between the egg halves. Next put a third egg half, filling side up, on top of the *ratatouille*. Sprinkle the eggs with the scallion.

Seafood Stuffed Eggs

4 servings

6 Hard-Cooked Eggs (page 35), halved
lengthwise

Sauce

The 6 hard-cooked egg yolks

1 cup heavy cream, approximately

1 tablespoon freshly squeezed lemon juice

¼ teaspoon freshly ground pepper

*I*n a small mixing bowl, mash the egg yolks. Add ¾ cup of the cream, the lemon juice, and the pepper and mix together thoroughly. Add more cream, a little at a time, until the sauce reaches napping consistency. Strain through a fine sieve and set aside.

Stuffing

1 cup cold cooked minced shellfish (shrimp, crab, or lobster)

½ cup peeled, seeded, and minced cucumber (1 small cucumber)

½ cup minced celery (½ a large stalk)

2 tablespoons chopped watercress leaves (6–7 sprigs)

3 tablespoons sour cream *or Crème Fraîche* (page 27)

1 teaspoon freshly squeezed lemon juice

¼ teaspoon grated lemon rind (avoid white pith, as it is bitter)

½ teaspoon salt

¼ teaspoon freshly ground pepper

1 bunch young watercress, stems removed

Mix together well the shellfish, cucumber, celery, chopped watercress leaves, sour cream, lemon juice, lemon rind, salt, and pepper. Stuff the egg-white halves by spreading one twelfth of the mixture evenly over the entire cut side of each one.

Assembly

Place one quarter of the watercress in the center of a luncheon plate. Place 3 egg halves, stuffing side down, in a pinwheel pattern on the watercress. Nap the eggs with one quarter of the sauce. Repeat for 3 more servings.

OMELETS

Basic Omelet

2 servings

4   extra-large eggs, at room temperature

⅛   teaspoon salt

     A scant ⅛ teaspoon freshly ground pepper

1   teaspoon heavy cream

2   tablespoons Clarified Butter (page 24)

1   teaspoon sweet butter, softened

     7-inch seasoned omelet pan with sloping sides

*Y*ou can use a nonstick skillet to help insure good results, as the omelet technique is awkward for the amateur to master. Preheat the oven to 450°F. Break the eggs into a small mixing bowl and add the salt, pepper, and cream. With a large fork, beat the eggs vigorously for about 30 seconds, or until they are well mixed but not frothy. In the omelet pan, over a medium-high flame, heat the clarified butter for 1 minute. Pour the egg mixture into the pan and, with the cooking fork, immediately begin to draw the cooked egg away from the sides of the pan into the center of the egg mass. (Try to keep the tines of the fork at a 45-degree angle to the bottom of the pan.) Slowly begin to agitate the pan backwards and forwards to prevent sticking. Now combine a vigorous back-and-forth shaking of the pan and rapid scrambling of the eggs. Do this until two thirds of the egg mass has formed a cohesive bond, which should take only about 30 seconds. Remove the pan from the heat and, with a final vigorous movement, shake the pan backwards and forwards again rapidly and simultaneously scramble until, in about 15 seconds, the edges of the omelet start to fold over, giving them a finished, rolled look all around. The center of the omelet should remain fairly loose and overall it should resemble a thick, moist pancake. At this point quickly and evenly distribute the omelet filling over one half of the omelet. Now slide a pancake turner around the sides and under the bottom of the omelet so that it will come easily out of the pan. Slide the spatula under the unfilled side and, with one quick stroke, keeping the spatula in place, slide the omelet onto an ovenproof plate and fold it over. After the omelet has come out of the oven, rub the surface with the softened butter.

For versatility, economy, and creativity in egg preparations nothing equals the scrambled French omelet. Well-chosen combinations of leftover meat, cheese, fish, and vegetables can become new, exciting resources for this all-embracing dish. In the fillings that follow, quantities are for individual 4-egg omelets. If other courses or side dishes are being served, one omelet can easily be sufficient for two.

Cheddar, Apple, and Sausage Omelet

1	thinly sliced cooked country sausage or sweet Italian sausage
⅓	cup grated sharp Cheddar cheese
½	green apple, peeled, cored, sliced thin, and sautéed in 1 tablespoon sweet butter, stirred or tossed over medium-high heat for about 1 minute

*K*eep the sausage and apples warm in a preheated 450°F. oven until the omelet is ready for filling. Reserve 3 slices of apple for garnish. Distribute apples, sausage, and cheese evenly over one half of the omelet and fold the omelet out onto an ovenproof plate. If no ovenproof plate is available, fold the omelet over in the pan. Slide the plate or pan into the oven just long enough for the cheese to melt, approximately 2 minutes. Remove the omelet from the oven and coat the surface with softened butter to make it shine and increase its buttery flavor.

Black Forest Ham and Brie Omelet

¼   cup (2 ounces) finely chopped Black Forest
      ham

3   tablespoons ripe Brie, rind removed

*F*ollow the instructions in the preceding recipe.

Tomato, Ricotta, Onions, Peppers, and Mozzarella Omelet

½   cup Tomato Sauce (page 25)

¼   cup ricotta cheese

¼   cup each onions and peppers, sautéed in
      1 tablespoon butter and seasoned with
      ⅛ teaspoon salt

1   ounce thinly sliced smoked (or fresh)
      mozzarella cheese

      Chopped parsley

*P*reheat the oven to 450°F. Heat the tomato sauce in a saucepan. Spread the ricotta over one side of the omelet. Drain the warm onions and peppers and distribute them evenly over the ricotta. Slide the omelet onto an ovenproof plate and fold. Drape slices of mozzarella cheese over the center of the omelet. Bake until the mozzarella melts, approximately 1 minute, pour sauce over or around omelet, and garnish with the parsley.

Roquefort, Watercress, and Bacon Omelet

¼ cup watercress leaves added to the egg mixture

1 tablespoon crumbled Roquefort cheese, mixed with 1 tablespoon plain or scallion cream cheese and 1 teaspoon *Crème Fraîche* (page 27) *or* sour cream

¼ cup warm crumbled cooked bacon (approximately 4 slices)

¼ cup sautéed watercress, drained and chopped (approximately 1 bunch, stems removed, sautéed in 1 tablespoon sweet butter, and lightly salted)

*P*reheat the oven to 450°F. Spread the Roquefort cheese mixture over one side of the omelet. Distribute the bacon and sautéed watercress over the cheese. Slide the omelet onto an ovenproof plate and fold it over. Place the omelet in the oven for approximately 45 seconds.

Smoked Salmon, Asparagus, and Fines Herbes Omelet

½ cup blanched chopped asparagus, mixed with ¼ teaspoon freshly squeezed lemon juice and 1 teaspoon sweet butter, melted

2 tablespoons finely chopped unsalted smoked salmon, mixed with 1 tablespoon finely minced fresh herbs (any combination of parsley, chives, dill, tarragon, basil)

*T*his filling can simply be spread evenly over the entire omelet, at which point the omelet is transferred to a warm plate, folded over, buttered, and garnished with a sprig of one of the fresh herbs. (Two tablespoons of sour cream or *Crème Fraîche* [page 27] may be used as an additional garnish with a lively looking sprig of fresh dill.)

Chèvre and Strawberry Omelet

⅓ cup sliced strawberries, sprinkled with ¼ teaspoon freshly squeezed lemon juice and ½ teaspoon sugar and sautéed for 30 seconds over high heat in 1 tablespoon sweet butter

¼ cup softened *chèvre* (goat) cheese mixed with 1 tablespoon sour cream

*P*reheat oven to 450°F. Add 1 teaspoon sugar to the egg mixture. (Keep the salt.) Mix the sautéed strawberries with the *chèvre* and place the mixture in the oven for 2–3 minutes. Spread the mixture over one half of the omelet. Slide the omelet onto an ovenproof plate and fold it over. Place the omelet in the oven for approximately 45 seconds.

SOUFFLÉS

*A*ll our soufflés are based on a master recipe (below), and the same steps are followed for each variation (starting on page 47). First, make the soufflé base, a béchamel to which egg yolks and flavorings are added. Then the oven is preheated and the soufflé dishes are prepared. Finally, the beaten egg whites are folded into the base. Remember that when you add cheese, it should always be incorporated into the soufflé base right after you have whisked in the egg yolks.

NOTE: Points to remember about egg whites for soufflés . . .

1. Separate the eggs carefully; the whites must contain no trace of yolk.

2. Wash and dry your equipment well before beating the whites; beater and bowl must not be oily or greasy.

3. Egg whites at room temperature will mount more voluminously than chilled ones; take your eggs out of the refrigerator 30 minutes before using. Do not attempt to beat egg whites in an already overheated kitchen; they will not rise to the lofty heights desired.

Master Soufflé Recipe

2 individual soufflés

Soufflé Base

1   tablespoon sweet butter

1   tablespoon all-purpose flour

⅔   cup heavy cream

2   extra-large egg yolks, at room temperature

Seasonings (see following recipes, pages 47–49)

*I*n a small saucepan, over a low flame, melt the butter. Remove the pan from the heat, add the flour, and stir with a small whisk for 1 minute. Return the pan to medium-low heat and gradually add the cream, stirring constantly until the mixture thickens. Remove from the heat, transfer to a bowl, and let cool. Then whisk in the egg yolks. At this point the flavorings (see the following recipes) should be added to the soufflé base. Remember that the base is to be incorporated into bland egg whites and should therefore be slightly overseasoned. Set the soufflé base aside.

To Complete the Soufflé Mixture

Softened sweet butter (to grease soufflé dishes)

2 tablespoons all-purpose flour (to flour soufflé dishes)

3 egg whites, at room temperature

A pinch of salt

¼ teaspoon cream of tartar (*optional*)

2 *soufflé dishes, 2-cup capacity each*

2 *pieces foil or parchment paper, 10 × 18 inches*

String

Preparing the Soufflé Dishes

Preheat the oven to 400°F. Rub the inside of the soufflé dishes with softened butter, sprinkle each one with 1 tablespoon of the flour, and swirl the dishes around to coat the sides and bottom thoroughly. Gently tap the sides of the soufflé dishes against the table to dislodge excess flour, turn them upside down, and shake. Fold the pieces of foil or parchment paper in half lengthwise and butter one side. Wrap and tie these "collars" (buttered side facing inward) around the outside of the dishes so that the collars rise 2½ to 3 inches above the rims. Set aside.

Preparing the Egg Whites

In an unlined copper bowl (preferably), with a balloon whisk, beat the egg whites slowly with a circular motion, vertically from the bottom of the bowl and up, until they begin to foam. Then add a pinch of salt (and the cream of tartar if you are not using a copper bowl). Using your lower arm and wrist muscles, gradually increase the speed, beating as much air as possible into the egg whites and rotating the bowl so that the whisk incorporates air into the entire mass. The whites are ready when firm, creamy (not dry) peaks just adhere easily to the whisk. (If you use an electric beater, beat at slow speed for about 1 minute, until the egg whites foam. Add the cream of tartar and salt. Gradually increase the speed to moderate while tilting the bowl and circulating the beater around the sides and up from the middle to beat as much air as possible into the mixture.)

Folding in the Egg Whites

Now the beaten egg whites are gently incorporated into the soufflé base so that they will retain as much of their volume as possible. This process is known as folding. First stir a big spoonful of egg whites into the soufflé base to lighten it. Then, with a rubber scraper, put the rest of the egg whites on top. Still using your rubber scraper, cut down from the top of the mixture to the bottom of the bowl, draw the scraper quickly toward you against the edge of the bowl and then up to the left and out. By this action, you are bringing a bit of the soufflé base from the bottom of the bowl up and over the egg whites. Continue the movement while slowly rotating the bowl until all the egg whites have been folded in, forming the finished soufflé mixture. The whole process should not take more than 1 minute. Do not attempt to be too thorough or to use a stirring motion, as it is better to leave a few unblended patches than to deflate the egg whites.

Baking and Serving the Soufflés

Gently scoop one half the soufflé mixture into each dish. Set the soufflé dishes in the center of the middle rack of the preheated oven. DO NOT OPEN THE OVEN DOOR FOR 15 MINUTES. Then take a quick look—the soufflés should have risen between 2 and 3 inches above the rim of the dishes. The ideal soufflé is one that has risen to its maximum height and browned lightly around the edges and the top surface. It should remain firm after the collar is carefully peeled away, yet still be very moist (almost the consistency of a thick sauce) in the center. For best results, serve immediately.

Prosciutto and Parmesan Soufflé

After adding the egg yolks to the soufflé base (page 45), add the following:

3   tablespoons freshly grated Parmesan cheese

⅓   cup minced sliced prosciutto, sautéed in 1 tablespoon sweet butter

    A large pinch of freshly grated nutmeg

1   tablespoon finely chopped parsley

¼   teaspoon salt

⅛   teaspoon freshly ground pepper

While the base is still hot, add the cheese, then add the remaining ingredients.

Mixed Vegetable Soufflé with Duxelles

*A*fter adding the egg yolks to the soufflé base (page 45), add the following:

2　tablespoons *chèvre* (goat) cheese (*optional*; see NOTE)

⅓　cup cooked mixed minced vegetables (carrot, cauliflower, and celery root are good choices), sautéed for 3–4 minutes in 2 tablespoons sweet butter, seasoned with ½ teaspoon minced garlic, ¼ teaspoon salt and ⅛ teaspoon freshly ground pepper, and drained

⅛　teaspoon freshly grated nutmeg

Duxelles

¾　cup minced raw mushrooms (*shiitake, morels, enok, chanterelles,* or field mushrooms)

1　small shallot, finely minced

1　tablespoon freshly squeezed lemon juice

1　tablespoon sweet butter

To prepare the *duxelles*, combine all the ingredients in a small pan and cook over low heat until all the liquid has evaporated.

NOTE: If you use the *chèvre* in this recipe, it is necessary to reduce the quantity of heavy cream in the soufflé base to ½ cup.

Smoked Salmon Soufflé
with Chives and Crème Fraîche

After adding the egg yolks to the soufflé base (page 45), add the following:

2   heaping tablespoons *Crème Fraîche* (*optional*, page 27; reduce heavy cream in soufflé base to ½ cup)

6   tablespoons (¼ pound) boned and minced smoked salmon

2   tablespoons finely chopped fresh chives

¼   teaspoon salt (if salmon is salty, use less)

⅛   teaspoon freshly ground black pepper

Seafood Soufflé

After adding the egg yolks to the soufflé base (page 45), add the following:

⅔   cup minced raw seafood (lobster, shrimp, scallops, sole)

1   teaspoon Madeira wine

1   tablespoon chopped fresh herbs

⅛   teaspoon freshly grated nutmeg

¼   teaspoon salt

⅛   teaspoon freshly ground pepper

Quiches,
Crêpes,
& Blintzes

QUICHES

Whatever type of quiche you make, the fundamental steps are the same. You make a *pâte brisée* shell, a basic quiche batter, and the filling of your choice. The sequence of assembly is the same. Each step is headed as if it were a separate recipe, with the different fillings given last, starting on page 55. The Leek Tart at the end of this section is made somewhat differently. Serve quiche warm but not oven-hot.

Pâte Brisée
One 8-inch pie shell

1   cup unbleached flour

½   teaspoon salt

¼   pound (1 stick) cold sweet butter, cut into small pieces

2   extra-large egg yolks

3   tablespoons cold water

  8-inch pie tin, 1½ inches deep

  Pastry board or cloth

  Rolling pin

  Dried beans or raw rice for weight

Into a medium-size bowl, sift the flour and salt together. Cut the cold butter into the flour with two knives until mixture forms crumbs like coarse cornmeal. This seems awkward until you do it a few times; the idea is to blend the two ingredients together as lightly as possible with the butter bits softening as little as possible. Success in this step helps insure a tender, flaky crust. Cut through and turn the mixture lightly over in the bowl until the largest pieces of butter are about the size of peas and there is about a handful of them.

Combine the egg yolks and water. Sprinkle the egg mixture over the flour mixture and stir gently with a fork until all is moistened evenly. There may be a few dry crumbs that are not incorporated long after the rest of the dough seems blended. Leave them; it is better to undermix than overmix, which toughens the pastry. With your fingertips, lightly gather and press dough into a ball. It does not have to be smooth-surfaced and homogeneous—just firmly and quickly pressed into an even ball. Wrap it in wax paper and chill in refrigerator for 2 hours or more. Let stand at room temperature for 30 minutes to make the dough soft enough to roll.

Preheat the oven to 450°F.

It is important to handle the dough gently throughout the entire rolling process to insure a tender pastry. Set the dough on a lightly floured surface and with the rolling pin roll it into a circle 12 to 13 inches in diameter. Unblended chunks of butter may stick to the board and rolling pin; simply scrape them away carefully with a pastry scraper or spatula, dust the damp spots on the board or rolling pin with flour, and continue rolling. Lift dough into pie tin and press it carefully into the bottom. Then lift the edges of the dough and work them gently down the inside edges of the pan with your fingers. (This guarantees a minimal amount of shrinkage during the "blind baking.") Prick the bottom of the shell with a fork at 1-inch intervals. Finish the edge with a pie-crust trim.

To keep the sides of the shell from collapsing and the bottom from puffing up, first line the shell with lightweight foil (or 2 sheets of wax paper). Press it well against the sides of the pastry and then fill it with the dried beans or rice. Bake in the middle of the oven for 8–10 minutes, or until the edges are slightly browned. Remove the pan from the oven.

Lower the oven temperature to 375°F.

Carefully remove the beans or rice and paper. Return the pan to the oven and bake for 5 minutes more, or until the crust is slightly opaque and less moist. At this point it is important to poke air out of any large blisters which may have risen in the crust. Remove from oven and set aside. This blind baking guarantees a crisp bottom crust.

Lower the oven temperature to 350°F.

❦

Basic Quiche Batter
One 8-inch quiche

1⅔   cups heavy cream

3   extra-large eggs

½   teaspoon salt (see NOTE)

¼   teaspoon freshly ground pepper

A pinch of cayenne pepper

3–4   grates nutmeg

NOTE: Eliminate salt for Westphalian Ham, Onion, and Brie Quiche (page 56).

*I*n a medium-size mixing bowl, combine all the ingredients thoroughly with a wire whisk.

This basic recipe yields enough batter to fill one quiche shell when it is added to the shell after the filling in any of the recipes that follow. The recipes are all designed for pie shells 8 inches in diameter, 1½ inches deep. However, there may be a slight excess, depending on individual variations in the shaping of the shell. Pour in only enough batter to reach a point ¼ inch below the rim.

The classic *quiche Lorraine* contains heavy cream, eggs, and bacon, but no cheese. We have developed variations that expand this basic concept. Here are a few examples of our style of quiche.

To Assemble a Quiche

*Y*our oven should be preheated to 350°F.

In a small mixing bowl, combine the grated Swiss or Fontina cheese and the filling in the recipe you have chosen. Distribute this mixture evenly over the crust. Slowly pour the quiche batter over the mixture. Gently move the filling and cheese with your finger so that the batter is evenly distributed, taking care not to poke a hole in the crust, as this will cause the liquid to run through and burn.

Bake the quiche in the center of the middle rack of the oven until the custard is set, approximately 50–60 minutes. To test the custard, make a small slit (1–2 inches long and 1 inch deep) in the center of the quiche. Place two fingers on either side of the opening and apply equal pressure on both sides. The custard is done when no liquid appears. Serve warm.

Smoked Salmon Quiche with Shallots and Fresh Herbs
4–6 servings

1   cup grated Swiss or Fontina cheese

4–5   ounces smoked salmon, finely chopped

2   tablespoons finely minced shallots

3   tablespoons chopped fresh herbs (Italian parsley, dill, chives)

Spinach, Bacon, and Mushroom Quiche
4–6 servings

1   cup grated Swiss or Fontina cheese

2   cups sliced raw mushrooms, sautéed in 2 tablespoons sweet butter and drained on paper towels

½   pound bacon, chopped and sautéed, drained on paper towels, and crumbled

5   ounces spinach, well washed and stems removed, briefly sautéed in 1 tablespoon sweet butter over medium-high heat, thoroughly squeezed to eliminate liquid, and chopped

Chicken and Broccoli Quiche
4–6 servings

1 cup grated Swiss or Fontina cheese

   A 1-pound chicken breast, cooked (When skinned and boned, this should yield 5 ounces of meat; cut into ½-inch cubes.)

1 teaspoon Madeira wine (sprinkled over chicken)

6 ounces blanched broccoli, chopped (about 2 cups)

Westphalian Ham, Onion, and Brie Quiche
4–6 servings

2 tablespoons grated Swiss or Fontina cheese

4 ounces Westphalian ham, chopped, slowly sautéed in 2 tablespoons sweet butter and drained thoroughly on paper towels

3 heaping tablespoons chopped onion, sautéed in 1 tablespoon fat from sautéed ham plus 1 tablespoon sweet butter

5 ounces Brie, rind removed

*B*efore assembling this quiche, blend the Brie and half the quiche batter in a food processor or a blender for 30 seconds.

Black Forest Ham Quiche
4–6 servings

1   cup grated Swiss or Fontina cheese

7   ounces Black Forest ham, finely chopped

¼   cup sautéed minced onion *(optional)*

Leek Tart
6–8 servings

1   "blind-baked" 8-inch Pie Shell (page 52)

Filling

2   cups thinly sliced white part of leek

2¼   cups thinly sliced yellow onions

¼   cup chopped shallots

1   teaspoon minced garlic

2   tablespoons finely chopped Italian parsley

½   teaspoon minced fresh rosemary

3   tablespoons soy oil

3   tablespoons sweet butter

½   teaspoon honey

1½   teaspoons salt

¼   teaspoon freshly ground pepper

2   tablespoons all-purpose flour

2   cups White Stock (page 116) *or* canned chicken stock

½   cup dry white wine

3   heaping tablespoons grated Swiss cheese

6   extra-large eggs beaten together with 1 tablespoon heavy cream

*I*n a heavy-bottomed saucepan, over a very low flame, sweat the leek, onions, shallots, garlic, parsley, and rosemary in the soy oil and butter, covered, for 15 minutes. Stir in the honey, salt, pepper, and flour and cook, uncovered, stirring frequently, for 30 minutes. Then add the stock and white wine, bring to a boil, lower to a simmer, and cook for another 30 minutes. Allow this mixture to cool.

Topping

¾   **cup thinly sliced leeks (white and light green parts)**

¾   **cup thinly sliced yellow onions**

2   **tablespoons sweet butter**

In a saucepan, over a very low flame, sweat the leeks and onions in the butter, covered, for 5–10 minutes, or until they are soft and tender. Set aside.

Preheat the oven to 350°F.

Combine the cooled filling mixture with the cheese and beaten eggs. Slowly pour the filling into the blind-baked shell; gently move the filling and eggs with your finger so that the batter is evenly distributed. Arrange the leek and onion topping over the filling. Bake the tart in the center of the middle rack of the oven until the custard is set, approximately 45 minutes. Serve warm.

CRÊPES

*W*e have adapted a classic *crêpe* recipe. It is slightly more complicated than the standard recipe found in most cookbooks, but we believe that the delicacy of flavor and lightness of texture of these *crêpes* make them worth the extra effort.

Crêpes
10 crêpes

½   **cup milk**

¼   **teaspoon salt**

2   **tablespoons sweet butter**

1¼   **cups unbleached flour, sifted before measuring**

¾   **teaspoon vegetable oil**

1   **extra-large egg**

⅓   **cup flat beer**

1–2   **teaspoons Clarified Butter (page 24)**

Fine-mesh sieve

7-inch crêpe pan

Preparing the Batter

In a small saucepan, over a low flame, heat the milk, salt, and the 2 tablespoons of butter until the butter has melted.

Put the flour into a medium bowl and make a well in the center. Pour the oil into the well and add the egg. Mix thoroughly by beating with a wire whisk, a somewhat difficult step because you are asked to incorporate all the dry ingredients with just a small amount of liquid. Pour in the warm milk mixture, stir in the beer, and mix until smooth. Strain the batter through the fine sieve and let it rest in the refrigerator for 2 hours before using.

Cooking the Crêpes

To cook the *crêpes*, place the *crêpe* pan or a well-seasoned omelet pan over moderate heat. Test the heat of the pan by flicking a few drops of water into it; they should sizzle. Your first *crêpe* will be a test. With a pastry brush or a paper towel, lightly brush the pan with a very small amount of the clarified butter. Spoon about 2 tablespoons of batter into the pan, then rotate the pan until the bottom is completely covered with a thin coating of batter. Tilt the pan immediately and pour the excess batter back into the bowl. Cook the *crêpe* for about 1 minute, or until the top loses its gloss and the *crêpe* can be easily lifted around the edge. With your fingers or a small spatula, flip the *crêpe* over, brown the other side for 30 seconds, and remove it to a plate. Stack the *crêpes*, separating them with sheets of wax paper. Continue cooking the *crêpes* until all the batter is used, buttering the pan sparingly as needed.

Storing the Crêpes

Wrap the stacked *crêpes* in foil and refrigerate for up to 2 days. To reheat, remove the *crêpes* from the refrigerator 30 minutes before you plan to put them in the oven. Preheat the oven to 450°F., place the *crêpes*, still in foil, on a baking sheet, and bake 2–3 minutes.

Spinach Crêpes
Approximately 10 crêpes

1¼	cups fresh spinach, well washed and stems removed
1⅛	cups milk
¾	cup unbleached flour, sifted before measuring
2	extra-large eggs
⅛	teaspoon salt
⅛	teaspoon freshly ground pepper
	A pinch of freshly grated nutmeg
2	tablespoons sweet butter, melted
	Food processor or *blender*
	7-inch crêpe pan

*B*ring 1 cup water to a boil, add the spinach, and blanch it until just wilted and still bright green, about 15 seconds. Drain in a colander and place under cold running water until it is thoroughly chilled. Drain the spinach and squeeze out all the remaining liquid. In the food processor or blender combine the spinach and milk and purée until the mixture is completely smooth. Add the remaining ingredients, except the butter, and blend thoroughly. Pour the mixture into a bowl, add the melted butter, and let the batter rest for about 2 hours.

To cook and store the *crêpes*, follow the instructions on pages 59–60.

Shrimp and
Smoked Salmon Crêpes with
Vermouth Cream Sauce
6 servings

6   Spinach *Crêpes* (page 60)

Filling

24   jumbo shrimp, peeled and deveined

6   ounces smoked salmon, coarsely chopped

1½   cups chopped raw asparagus, zucchini, *or* spinach *(optional)*

Salt to taste

¾   teaspoon freshly ground pepper

2   tablespoons finely chopped fresh chives

2   tablespoons finely chopped fresh dill

Vermouth Cream Sauce
Makes about 3¾ cups

1½   cups dry vermouth

3   cups heavy cream

3   cups Fish Stock (page 118)

2   tablespoons freshly squeezed lemon juice

6   *ovenproof plates* or *1 large ovenproof serving dish*

Make the sauce: Combine all the sauce ingredients in a 10- to 12-inch stainless-steel or enameled skillet and cook over medium-low heat until reduced by half. Add the seafood, vegetables, and salt and pepper and continue to simmer the mixture until the shrimp are cooked, about 2–3 minutes. Add the herbs and remove from the heat.

Preheat the oven to 300°F. Place 1 *crêpe* on each ovenproof plate. Carefully arrange 4 shrimp on one half of the *crêpe*, spoon over them a sixth of the vegetables and 1–2 tablespoons of the sauce, and fold over the other half of the *crêpe*. (When all the *crêpes* are filled, there should be about 1½ cups of sauce left.) Bake the *crêpes* for 3–5 minutes, just to heat them. Reheat the sauce, nap each *crêpe* with a large spoonful of it, and serve immediately.

Crêpes Italienne with Tomato Sauce

6 servings

6	Spinach *Crêpes* (page 60)
½	cup olive oil
¾	pound prosciutto, cut into ¼-inch dice
¾	cup minced red or green bell pepper
¾	teaspoon minced garlic
¾	teaspoon minced onion
¾	cup minced mushrooms
¾	pound pepperoni sausage, cut into ¼-inch dice, or crumbled Italian sausage
3	cups Tomato Sauce (page 25)
1½	cups Beaujolais wine or dry vermouth
	Salt and freshly ground pepper to taste
1	cup ricotta cheese
6	thin slices mozzarella cheese
6	*ovenproof plates* or *1 large ovenproof serving dish*

*P*reheat the oven to 400°F. In a 10- to 12-inch stainless-steel or enameled skillet, heat the oil. Add the prosciutto, peppers, garlic, onion, and mushrooms and sauté over moderate heat until the onion and peppers are soft. Add the pepperoni and cook until heated through, then pour off the excess fat. Add the tomato sauce and wine and simmer and reduce the sauce for 10–15 minutes. Correct the seasoning with salt and pepper.

Place a spinach *crêpe* on an ovenproof plate. Spread about 1½ tablespoons of the ricotta mixture over half the *crêpe*, roll into a tube, and cover with a slice of mozzarella. Continue filling the *crêpes* until all are used. Bake the *crêpes* until the cheese has melted, about 4–5 minutes. While the *crêpes* are baking, reheat the sauce in the skillet. When the *crêpes* are ready, place a large spoonful of sauce over each and serve immediately.

Lamb Curry Crêpes
4–6 servings

6   *Crêpes* (page 59)

Lamb Stock
Makes about 5 cups

Bones from 1 lamb shoulder

2   tomatoes, chopped

1   stalk celery, chopped

½   yellow onion, coarsely chopped

1   large carrot, coarsely chopped

2   teaspoons kosher *or* sea salt

3   white peppercorns

3   cloves garlic

2   bay leaves

½   teaspoon fresh rosemary or a pinch of dry rosemary

Stock pot

Food processor *or* **blender**

*P*reheat the oven to 450°–500°F.

Put the bones, tomatoes, celery, onion, and carrot on a baking sheet and roast until dark brown in color, approximately 45 minutes. Transfer the ingredients to a stock pot and cover with cold water. Add the salt and add the remaining ingredients wrapped in cheesecloth. Bring to a boil, lower the heat, and simmer, skimming as necessary, for 1½–2 hours. Strain the stock in a colander and skim off any grease. Discard the lamb bones.

Remove the herb pouch from the vegetables and purée the vegetables in the food processor or blender or by forcing them through a sieve. Reserve the stock and the purée separately.

Lamb Curry

1½	pounds boneless lamb shoulder, cut into 2-inch pieces
5	cups Lamb Stock
3	tablespoons sweet butter
1	onion, thinly sliced
2	stalks celery, diced
5	small cloves garlic, crushed in a mortar and pestle with 1½ teaspoons cuminseeds
1½	teaspoons salt
½	teaspoon dry mustard
	A pinch of cayenne pepper
¼	teaspoon ground coriander
¼	teaspoon ground mace
1	tablespoon medium-strength curry powder
	Puréed stock vegetables
3	cups heavy cream
¾	cup currants
2	tart unpeeled apples, cored and cut into ¼-inch slices
	Juice of 1 lime

Optional garnish:

½   cup plain yogurt

6   tablespoons slivered or sliced amonds,
     toasted for 10 minutes in a preheated 350°F.
     oven

     6-quart pot

     *4–6 ovenproof plates or 1 large ovenproof
     serving dish*

In the pot, combine the lamb and the stock, bring to a boil, lower the
heat, and simmer for approximately 1½ hours, or until the meat is fork-tender.

Melt the butter in a 10- to 12-inch stainless-steel or enameled skillet over
a medium flame, add the onion, celery, garlic, and all the spices, and sauté
until the vegetables begin to turn a golden brown, about 5 minutes. Remove
from the heat and set aside.

When the lamb has finished cooking, remove the meat from the stock,
shred it into bite-size pieces, and set aside. Reduce the stock by one third. Add
the puréed vegetables to the reduced stock. Transfer this mixture to the skillet
with the cream and currants. Cook over medium heat for 5–10 minutes, then
add the lamb meat, apple slices, and lime juice.

Preheat the oven to 300°F.

Put 1 *crêpe* on each ovenproof plate. Put ¾ cup lamb curry over half the
crêpe and fold over the other half. Continue filling *crêpes* until all are used, then
bake for 3–5 minutes, until heated through. To finish, spoon the remaining
sauce over the *crêpes*, top with a dollop of yogurt, if desired, and sprinkle with
the almonds. Serve immediately.

Duck Crêpes
4–6 servings

3   duck breasts, roasted in a preheated 400°F. oven for 20 minutes or 1½ pounds cooked duck meat, boned and skinned

1   quart Duck Stock (page 117) *or* White Stock (page 116)

1½ cups freshly squeezed orange juice

6   tablespoons sherry vinegar

¾   teaspoon green peppercorns

36 orange sections, peel, membrane, and seeds removed (page 105)

¾   teaspoon orange rind, blanched and cut into julienne strips

½   cup apple purée *or* applesauce

Additional thin slices of roasted duck meat *(optional)*

4–6 *Crêpes* (page 59)

4–6 *ovenproof plates*

*I*n a 10- to 12-inch stainless-steel or enameled skillet, combine the stock, orange juice, vinegar, and green peppercorns. Over a medium-low flame, reduce this mixture by one third. Reheat the duck meat in the sauce, remove it from the pan, and turn off the heat. Slice the duck meat very thin and return it to the sauce with the orange sections, rind, and apple purée.

Preheat the oven to 300°F. Put 1 *crêpe* on each ovenproof plate. Place approximately ¾ cup of the duck meat and oranges together with 1–2 tablespoons of the sauce on half of the *crêpe* and fold over the *crêpe*. Continue filling the crêpes until all are used. Bake for 3–5 minutes, until just heated through. Finish by napping each *crêpe* with a large spoonful of sauce and garnish with a few additional small slices of roasted duck meat, if desired. Serve immediately.

NOTE: The duck carcass and legs may be used for the duck stock or for Duck Pâté (page 146).

Smoked Turkey or Smoked Chicken Crêpes with Madeira Cream Sauce

6 servings

6   *Crêpes* (page 59)

1½ pounds smoked turkey or smoked chicken, skinned and cut into small bite-size pieces

5½ tablespoons sweet butter

1½ unpeeled green apples, cored and cut into ¼-inch slices

2   teaspoons minced onions

¼   cup plus 2 heaping tablespoons pecans or walnuts

¾   teaspoon salt

Madeira Cream Sauce

3   cups heavy cream

3   cups White Stock (page 116) *or* canned chicken stock

6   tablespoons Madeira or Port wine

¾   teaspoon salt

¾   teaspoon freshly ground pepper

6   *ovenproof plates*

*I*n a 10-inch stainless-steel or enameled skillet, melt the butter over a medium flame. Sauté the apples, onions, and nuts until golden, then season with the salt. Transfer this mixture to a mixing bowl and set aside.

In a 10- to 12-inch stainless-steel or enameled skillet, combine all the sauce ingredients and, over medium-low heat, reduce by one third. Add the turkey and the apple mixture and heat through—about 5 minutes.

Preheat the oven to 300°F. Put 1 *crêpe* on each ovenproof plate. Put approximately ¾ cup of the turkey and apple mixture together with 1–2 tablespoons of the sauce over one half the *crêpe* and fold the *crêpe* over. Continue filling the *crêpes* until all are used. Bake for 3–5 minutes, until just heated through. Finish by spooning the remaining sauce, apples, and nuts over the *crêpes*. Serve immediately.

BLINTZES

To Make Blintzes

10 blintzes, approximately 6 inches in diameter

½	cup milk
¼	cup water
2	small eggs or 1 extra-large egg
¾	cup unbleached flour, sifted before measuring
¼	teaspoon salt
1½	tablespoons sweet butter, melted
	Clarified Butter (page 24), to grease *crêpe* pan
2–4	tablespoons clarified butter to sauté filled blintzes
	Food processor
	6-inch *crêpe* pan

Preparing the Batter

To make the batter by hand, beat the milk, water, and eggs in a mixing bowl, add the flour and salt, and beat until well blended. Stir in the melted butter.

To make the batter with a food processor, add the liquid ingredients to the processor bowl and blend for 3–5 seconds. Add the flour and salt and process until smooth.

Blintz batter can be used as soon as it is made.

Cooking the Blintzes

Follow the instructions for cooking *crêpes* (page 59), using a 6-inch *crêpe* pan. Cook the blintzes *on one side only*, as they will be cooked again after they are filled.

Filling and Rolling the Blintzes

Lay each blintz out flat, cooked side up, and put about ⅓ cup filling in the center. Fold the bottom of the blintz up over the filling so that the bottom edge is 1½ inches from the top edge. Press the filling into a tube shape, taking care that it does not ooze out. Fold the sides in to form a pouch and start rolling the blintz very carefully, tucking in the corners as you go until you have a cylinder about 3 inches long and 1 inch wide.

Browning the Filled Blintzes

The filled blintzes can be finished either by being sautéed or baked.

To sauté, heat the clarified butter in 1 or 2 heavy frying pans, put the blintzes in the pan seam side down, and sauté, turning them carefully, until golden brown in all sides.

To bake, preheat the oven to 450°F. Brush an ovenproof serving dish large enough to hold all the blintzes in one layer with the clarified butter. Put the blintzes in the dish seam side down, brush with the butter, and bake 10 minutes, or until golden brown. Serve immediately.

Seafood Blintzes
with Vermouth Cream Sauce
4 servings

¼	pound fillet of sole, cut into ½-inch pieces
4–5	large undercooked shrimp, peeled and deveined
2	tablespoons finely minced white of leek
½	cup White Stock (page 116) *or* Fish Stock (page 118)
2	tablespoons sweet butter
½	shallot, finely minced
1	teaspoon minced fresh chives
½	teaspoon finely minced scallion
2	teaspoons chopped Italian parsley
2	teaspoons chopped fresh dill
2	teaspoons dry vermouth
2	teaspoons egg white, lightly beaten
¼	teaspoon salt
4–5	grinds fresh pepper
	A pinch of cayenne pepper
	A pinch of fresh grated nutmeg
8	cooked Blintzes (see *preceding recipe*)
1	recipe warm Vermouth Cream Sauce (page 61)

In a small skillet, over medium heat, cook the leek in the stock until tender, approximately 4–5 minutes. Remove the leek with a slotted spoon, place in a medium bowl, and cool. Melt the butter in the skillet. Briefly poach the shallot, chives, and scallion for 15–30 seconds, add the sole, and cook until it is just tender, about 30 seconds. With the slotted spoon, remove the sole and shallot and set aside to cool with the leek. Using the large holes of a hand grater, grate the shrimp into the leek and sole mixture, add the remaining ingredients, and mix thoroughly. Add the poaching liquid to the reduced vermouth cream sauce.

Fill and brown the blintzes following the instructions on page 69. Serve with the sauce.

Potato Blintzes

4 servings

8   cooked Blintzes (page 68)

Filling

¾   pound new potatoes, peeled

1⅛   teaspoons salt, in all

2   teaspoons finely minced scallions

1   teaspoon finely minced fresh chives

1   tablespoon sour cream

1   teaspoon *Crème Fraîche* (page 27)

1   teaspoon sweet butter, melted

4–5   grinds pepper

A pinch of freshly grated nutmeg

A pinch of cayenne pepper

½   cup sour cream, mixed with 2 teaspoons chopped fresh chives and salt and pepper to taste

Potato ricer or food mill with medium blade

*I*n a large saucepan, cover the potatoes with water, add 1 teaspoon of the salt, and bring to a boil. Lower the flame to a medium simmer and cook until the potatoes are easily pierced with a fork, approximately 40 minutes. Cool. Pass the potatoes through the ricer or food mill into a mixing bowl, add the remaining filling ingredients, and mix thoroughly. Fill and brown the blintzes following the instructions on page 69. Garnish each blintz with a tablespoon of the sour cream mixture and serve immediately.

Vegetable Blintzes
2 servings

4 cooked Blintzes (page 68)

Filling

1 cup farmer cheese

2 tablespoons minced carrot

1 tablespoon minced scallion

2 tablespoons diced red bell pepper

2 teaspoons minced fresh chives

¼ teaspoon salt

⅛ teaspoon freshly ground pepper

1 tablespoon minced watercress leaves

1 tablespoon chopped parsley

½ cup sour cream, mixed with 2 teaspoons chopped fresh chives and salt and pepper to taste

*I*n a small mixing bowl, combine all the filling ingredients. Fill and brown the blintzes following the instructions on page 69. Garnish with the sour cream mixture.

Apple Blintzes
4 servings

8   cooked Blintzes (page 68)

Filling

4   apples, peeled, cored, and sliced ¼ inch
     thick

2   tablespoons sweet butter

2½   tablespoons brown sugar

1   teaspoon salt

     A pinch of ground cloves

     A pinch of ground cinnamon

     A pinch of freshly grated nutmeg

4   heaping tablespoons currants

¼   cup heavy cream *or* apple juice

Sour Cream Topping

2½   cups sour cream

     A pinch of freshly grated nutmeg

     A pinch of ground cinnamon

     A pinch of ground cloves

     A small squeeze of fresh lemon juice

1   tablespoon brown sugar

     Optional garnishes:

¼   cup chopped toasted almonds

½   teaspoon grated lemon rind

*I*n a skillet, over a medium-low flame, melt the butter. Add the remaining filling ingredients, except the cream, sauté until the apples are golden brown and tender, approximately 5–10 minutes, and transfer to a bowl to cool. Deglaze the pan with the cream or apple juice and add to bowl. Fill and brown the blintzes following the instructions on page 69.

Mix the topping ingredients together in a bowl, spoon liberally over the blintzes, and sprinkle with the almonds and lemon rind. Serve immediately.

Peach Blintzes

4 servings

8   cooked Blintzes (page 68)

1   recipe Sour Cream Topping (see *preceding recipe*)

4   tablespoons sweet butter

2   tablespoons finely chopped onion

½   teaspoon finely minced garlic

2   teaspoons honey

2   teaspoons sugar

     A pinch of ground mace

2   teaspoons sherry vinegar

¼   teaspoon salt

4   large peaches, peeled, pitted, and coarsely chopped (approximately 1½ cups)

*I*n a skillet, over a medium flame, melt the butter. Sauté the onion and garlic for 2–3 minutes, or until the onion is soft, and add the remaining ingredients. Cook until the peaches are tender, approximately 5 minutes. Chill briefly.

Fill and brown the blintzes following the instructions on page 69. Divide the topping among the blintzes and serve immediately.

Salads

*F*or many years an active fantasy of ours has been to relocate the Charcuterie in an area surrounded by farmland, where the climate supports a long growing season and where we could learn how our own fruits and vegetables are grown and how livestock is raised. However, our being loyal New Yorkers interferes with the realization of that dream and explains why we rejoice when the first spring asparagus poke their heads out of the warming earth. It is a sign of regional bounty unfolding. Throughout the spring, summer, and fall we travel to Connecticut, New Jersey, and Long Island farms to select the ingredients for our salads, soups, and vegetables to cook and for *crudités*. We buy fertilized eggs from local farmers and real, unadulterated cream to lavish on strawberries. We are passionate about maintaining the integrity of the pure ingredient on its way from the field to the table.

We prepare all the salads at the restaurant fresh daily, basing them on seasonal availability of ingredients. Although the vegetables in these recipes may appear in the markets all year round, they are not always at their peak. We may not be able to control the expansion of mass-produced eggs, fruits, vegetables, chickens, meats, and so on in this country, but we can always be aware and discriminating shoppers. For example, celebrate the summer corn harvest by using freshly picked ears to produce the corn salads and never try to adapt the recipes in the winter with the canned or frozen variety; prepare the Marinated Mushroom salad instead. There is enough of a selection to enable you always to use ingredients at their peak!

Our term "life-span" is the length of time a particular salad is at its freshest. Since the Charcuterie attaches a price tag to its food, we serve our customers as you would your guests. That is why we indicate serving immediately or brief life-spans for certain salads.

Vinaigrette
Makes 1¾ cups

1 teaspoon beaten egg yolk

2 tablespoons tarragon vinegar or sherry
   vinegar

1 tablespoon freshly squeezed lemon juice

1 teaspoon Dijon mustard

½ teaspoon salt

¼ teaspoon freshly ground pepper

1 cup soy oil

⅓ cup olive oil

For a walnut- or hazelnut-flavored vinaigrette, substitute 2 tablespoons walnut
or hazelnut oil for 2 tablespoons soy oil, and eliminate the olive oil.

Optional:

1 heaping teaspoon chopped parsley

1 teaspoon chopped fresh chives

1 teaspoon chopped fresh dill

*P*lace all the ingredients except the oils in a mixing bowl.
With a small or medium whisk, combine thoroughly, using a rapid wrist motion. While whisking, add the oils, in a slow steady stream, incorporating them
slowly to guarantee that the dressing emulsifies. Whisk in the desired herbs and
taste for seasoning.

Mayonnaises

*W*e have tended to use the food processor to make may-
onnaise for our salads at the Charcuterie, since it makes quantity production
easier. However, sometimes it seems just as easy for home portions (in most

cases 1½ cups or less) to make it by hand, in a bowl with a whisk.

We season mayonnaises in many different ways, depending on the salads in which they are used. This means that you proceed a little differently for processor mayonnaise or one made by hand.

With either method, be sure all ingredients are at room temperature.

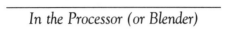

In the Processor (or Blender)

In the container, place the egg yolks, vinegar, and all the seasonings of the particular mayonnaise and purée for approximately 15 seconds, until the mixture is frothy. Then add the oil in a steady stream, slowly at first, until it is all incorporated. If there is an addition of cream, it is stirred in at the last, as are any chopped ingredients that should not be puréed in the processor.

By Hand

In a bowl, whisk together well the yolk(s) and vinegar until the mixture is frothy. Then, drop by drop, whisk in the oil until the mixture begins to thicken, at which point you may start to add the remaining oil in a slow steady stream. When the mayonnaise is ready, stir in the herbs and other seasonings. Any ingredients that require chopping should be finely minced, since there is no chopping blade at work during the making of the mayonnaise.

Rather than repeating these instructions in all the recipes, we refer you to this page. You will see that we do recommend that a food processor be used in certain recipes. However, this is not essential.

If your mayonnaise breaks down during construction, you can reconstitute it. Whisk together an egg yolk and a dash of vinegar or lemon juice in a clean bowl and into this whisk the mayonnaise, a little at a time.

Homemade mayonnaises tend to keep well only for 3–5 days, after which the flavors may change. Store, tightly covered, in the refrigerator.

NOTE: Extra-large eggs, or at least large eggs, should be used in all our mayonnaise recipes.

Green Beans with Pears, Pine Nuts, and Chèvre

4 servings

¾   pound young green beans, ends removed

1½   ripe pears (Bosc or Anjou tend to hold shape best)

⅓   cup pine nuts, toasted for 10 minutes in a preheated 350°F. oven

Vinaigrette

1   tablespoon tarragon vinegar

1½   teaspoons freshly squeezed lemon juice

1½   teaspoons Dijon mustard

½   teaspoon salt

¼   teaspoon freshly ground pepper

½   cup soy oil

2   tablespoons olive oil

¼   cup moist *chèvre* (goat) cheese, crumbled

*B*lanch the green beans in boiling salted water (1 teaspoon of salt to a gallon of water) for 1½ minutes. Drain in a colander and place under cold running water, or plunge into ice water until cool. Allow to drain thoroughly. Pat dry.

Halve and core the pears and slice lengthwise ¼ inch thick. Combine the beans, pears, and pine nuts in a mixing bowl.

Make the vinaigrette following the instructions on page 76, pour it over the bean mixture, and sprinkle with the *chèvre*. Toss gently. This salad is best served immediately or chilled for only 30 minutes.

Life-span: 6 hours, well covered, in the refrigerator; past this point, the color of the beans fades and the texture becomes soggy.

Marinated Beets

6 servings

1½	pounds small to medium beets, stems trimmed to ½ inch
2	tablespoons brown sugar
2	cups tarragon vinegar
1	clove garlic, peeled

Spices Tied in a Piece of Washed Cheesecloth

5–6	cloves
1	teaspoon crushed black peppercorns
10–12	whole allspice
¼	teaspoon coriander seeds
12–14	juniper berries
¼	teaspoon caraway seeds
2	bay leaves

*P*reheat the oven to 350°F. In a large baking pan bake the beets until tender, when they can be easily pierced with a fork, from 1–2 hours, depending on size. (See NOTE.) Place under cold running water to cool. Peel off the skins, cut off the roots, and trim the remaining stems. Quarter the beets, or, if they are small, leave them whole. In a stainless-steel or enameled saucepan large enough to hold the beets, over a low flame, dissolve the sugar in the vinegar, and add the garlic and spice bag. Bring the marinade to a boil and simmer very slowly for 5 minutes. Add the beets and simmer, stirring frequently, for 10 more minutes. Transfer the beets and marinade to a bowl and cool to room temperature. Marinate the beets for 12 hours, either refrigerated or at room temperature.

Life-span: 7 days, well covered, in the refrigerator

NOTE: Baking as opposed to boiling is a slower process, but it is worth the wait; the beet flavor is concentrated and the color is sublime.

Broccoli with Garlic Mayonnaise

4–6 servings

2	bunches young broccoli, lower stem ends removed
2	teaspoons salt

Cut the broccoli tops into flowerets. Cut the stems into ½-inch slices. Add the salt to 2 gallons of boiling water, add the broccoli, and blanch for 1½ minutes. Drain the broccoli in a colander and place under cold running water until cool. Drain thoroughly. Pat dry any remaining water to insure that the mayonnaise adheres to the vegetable.

Garlic Mayonnaise

	Pulp of 3 large cloves Roasted Garlic (see *following recipe*)
2	extra-large egg yolks
1	tablespoon freshly squeezed lemon juice
	Grated zest ½ lemon
2	anchovy fillets, washed, reserving 1
2	tablespoons freshly grated Parmesan cheese
1	tablespoon tarragon vinegar
¾	teaspoon salt
½	teaspoon freshly ground black pepper
¾	cup soy oil
2	tablespoons olive oil
2	tablespoons heavy cream
	Food processor

Place all the ingredients in the food processor, except the oils, cream, and reserved anchovy. Purée for approximately 15 seconds, then add the oils in a slow steady stream. When oils are fully incorporated, add the cream.

In a mixing bowl, combine the mayonnaise and broccoli. Mince the reserved anchovy, add to the bowl, and stir together well. Check seasoning. Serve immediately or chill.

Life-span: for the mayonnaise, 48 hours, well covered, in the refrigerator; the salad must be served within 6 hours, as broccoli discolors.

Roasted Garlic
1 head

1   **whole head garlic, unpeeled**
1   **tablespoon olive oil**

*P*reheat the oven to 300°F. Prepare the garlic by cutting out the root and removing as much of the papery outer covering as possible. Do not remove the individual cloves, however, and do not peel them. Coat the garlic with the oil, wrap it in aluminum foil, and roast until the cloves are easily pierced with a fork, approximately 2 hours. Let the garlic cool and separate the cloves. To obtain the pulp, squeeze it out of the skins and then discard them. Store unused roasted cloves (they are by now a purée) in a tightly covered container in the refrigerator.

Life-span: 1 month, well covered, in the refrigerator

Carrots with Rosemary

6 servings

1½	pounds finger or young Belgian carrots or 2 pounds tender long carrots, scrubbed and unpeeled
1½	tablespoons olive oil
2	cloves garlic, crushed
½	teaspoon salt
	A 3–4-inch sprig fresh rosemary
2	teaspoons red-wine vinegar
1	tablespoon sherry vinegar
2	teaspoons freshly squeezed lemon juice
1½	tablespoons peanut or olive oil
1	teaspoon kosher salt
¼	teaspoon freshly ground black pepper
¼	teaspoon finely minced fresh rosemary
⅛	teaspoon finely minced garlic
½	teaspoon chopped Italian parsley

*P*our 1½ tablespoons olive oil into a sauté pan, add the crushed garlic, and heat over a low flame until odor of garlic begins to waft into your nostrils, 7–10 minutes. When garlic begins to brown, remove and discard. Pour oil into a mixing bowl large enough to hold the carrots.

Cut the carrots slightly on the diagonal into thin oval slices. Bring 1 gallon of water and ½ teaspoon salt to a boil, add the carrots and the rosemary sprig, and cook until the carrots are tender, about 5–10 minutes, depending on their size. (Remove when slightly underdone, since they will continue to cook for several minutes while draining.) Drain well and combine with the garlic-flavored oil. Add the remaining ingredients while the carrots are still hot and toss well; the hot carrots tend to soak up the flavors better. Serve warm or cold.

Life-span: 2 days, well covered, in the refrigerator

Assembly of Grated Vegetable Salads

Put all the salad ingredients through the shredding disk of the food processor, except the walnuts and currants in Grated Salad II, which should be mixed in after the other ingredients have been grated. Transfer the shredded vegetables to a medium-size bowl and mix them thoroughly. For Grated Salads I and II, sprinkle the ingredients for the respective dressings over the vegetables, then combine thoroughly. Refrigerate or serve immediately, using a slotted spoon as there may be extra liquid.

Grated Salad I
4–6 servings

½   pound carrots

¼   pound parsnips, peeled

2   ounces red cabbage

Dressing

¼   cup freshly squeezed orange juice

1   tablespoon julienne orange peel, blanched in boiling water for 30 seconds, rinsed in cold water, and patted dry

2   teaspoons freshly squeezed lemon juice

1   tablespoon sherry vinegar

¼   cup soy oil

3   tablespoons olive oil

½   teaspoon salt

¼   teaspoon freshly ground pepper

Grated Salad II
4–6 servings

½   pound carrots

2   ounces parsnips, peeled

2   ounces celery root, peeled (see NOTE)

2   ounces red cabbage

⅓   cup walnuts, broken into pieces

2   heaping tablespoons currants

Dressing

2   tablespoons sherry vinegar

1   teaspoon freshly squeezed lemon juice

¼   cup soy oil

1   tablespoon walnut oil

½   teaspoon salt

¼   teaspoon freshly ground pepper

Grated Salad III
4–6 servings

½   pound carrots

2   ounces celery root, peeled (see NOTE)

¼   pound zucchini, washed

Dressing

⅛   teaspoon finely minced garlic

2   teaspoons Dijon mustard

2   tablespoons tarragon vinegar

1   teaspoon freshly squeezed lemon juice

¼   cup olive oil

½   teaspoon salt

¼   teaspoon freshly ground pepper

1   tablespoon chopped fresh herbs

Mix together thoroughly the garlic, mustard, vinegar, and lemon juice. Gradually add the oil and the remaining ingredients.

Life-span: Once dressed, the salad's texture starts to soften; in 6 hours it will be soggy.

NOTE: Leftover peeled celery root should be rubbed with lemon juice. It can be stored in the vegetable bin of the refrigerator for 2 days and used in Cream of Celery Root Soup, page 130.

Corn Salad I
6–8 servings

8–10	ears newly picked corn, shucked
2	cups milk
1	teaspoon kosher salt
½	teaspoon salt
¼	teaspoon freshly ground black pepper
¼	cup julienne strips of leek, white and pale green parts only
¾	cup finely diced red bell pepper
¾	cup julienne strips of carrot
¼	cup minced fresh chives
¾	cup Italian plum tomatoes, peeled, seeded, and minced
½	cup minced radishes
2	tablespoons chopped Italian parsley
⅓	cup Mayonnaise

Mayonnaise
Makes about ¾ cup

1   extra-large egg yolk

1   tablespoon tarragon vinegar

½   cup soy oil

2   tablespoons olive oil

1½   teaspoons freshly squeezed lemon juice

1   teaspoon salt

⅛   teaspoon freshly ground pepper

6   leaves fresh basil, finely chopped

*F*ollow the instructions for making mayonnaise by hand, page 77.

To prepare the corn: Cut the ears in half crosswise. Place the flat end of each piece on a chopping board and, with a broad knife, cut straight down, not too deep, to remove the kernels.

In a medium-size heavy-bottomed saucepan, bring 4 cups water, the milk, and salt to a boil. Add the corn kernels, turn down the heat, and cook for approximately 5–7 minutes, or until the kernels are just tender, still slightly undercooked. Drain the corn immediately, spread it out on a plate to cool, and sprinkle it with the salt and pepper. In a medium-size mixing bowl, gently combine the corn with the remaining ingredients, mixing thoroughly. Serve chilled. This salad is best served the same day.

Life-span: 24 hours, well covered, in the refrigerator

Corn Salad II

8–10 servings

Kernels from 8 ears white or golden corn
(3½–4 cups)

4½ cups inexpensive dry champagne or white
wine

2 roasted red or green bell peppers (page 88),
cut into strips 1 × ⅛ inch

4 sun-dried tomatoes (Pumate San Remo),
drained and minced *or* 2 marinated fresh
plum tomatoes (see NOTE)

½ cup olive oil from the sun-dried tomatoes or
plain olive oil

2 heaping tablespoons minced fresh chives

½ teaspoon salt

Freshly ground pepper to taste

*B*ring 4 cups of the champagne to a simmer in a medium-size saucepan, add the corn, and cook at a simmer for 5–7 minutes, or until the kernels are just tender, still slightly undercooked. Drain, spread the corn out on a plate to cool, and sprinkle with the remaining champagne. Transfer the corn to a serving bowl, add the remaining ingredients, and combine gently but thoroughly. Stir occasionally, if you are not serving the salad immediately.

Life-span: 24 hours, well covered, in the refrigerator

NOTE: To marinate the plum tomatoes, cut them into ¼-inch dice and combine with 1 teaspoon freshly squeezed lemon juice, ¼ teaspoon salt, ½ cup olive oil, and freshly ground pepper to taste. Marinate overnight and drain well before adding to the salad.

To Roast Bell Peppers

*U*sing kitchen tongs, hold the red or green bell pepper over a gas flame, turning it until the skin crackles and turns black. Or, roast the pepper on a baking sheet in a preheated 550°F. oven for 10 minutes. When all the skin has turned black, plunge the pepper into cold water; the skin will slip off easily. Remove the stem and scoop out the seeds.

Cucumbers with Dill and Sour Cream
8 servings

1¾   pounds cucumbers

2   teaspoons kosher salt

*P*eel the cucumbers and cut off the ends. Slice the cucumbers in half lengthwise and with a teaspoon, scrape out the pulp and seeds. Slice each half crosswise into crescents ⅛ by ¼ inch thick. Place in a sieve, sprinkle with the salt, toss to distribute the salt. Drain for 30 minutes. (The salt will draw out any excess water and bitterness that later could affect the dressing.) To insure dryness, pat or roll the cucumbers dry on or between paper towels or cloth napkins.

Sour Cream Dressing

1   tablespoon freshly squeezed lemon juice

¼   teaspoon freshly ground pepper

⅔   cup sour cream

1   rounded tablespoon chopped fresh dill

2   teaspoons chopped fresh chives

3   tablespoons grated fresh horseradish

2   tablespoons chopped radish *(optional)*

2   tablespoons thinly sliced scallions *(optional)*

In a small mixing bowl, stir the lemon juice and pepper into the sour cream with the herbs and horseradish. Gently fold the dressing and radish and scallions, if used, into the cucumbers, and chill for 30 minutes.

Life-span: 6 hours, well covered, in the refrigerator. If kept longer, the salad becomes soggy.

Cucumber Salad with Lime

6–8 servings

1¾	pounds cucumbers
2	limes
1	teaspoon white-wine or tarragon vinegar
4	cloves garlic, gently smashed and peeled
½	teaspoon sugar
¼	teaspoon ground coriander
	A pinch of cayenne pepper
1	teaspoon salt
1	tablespoon chopped Italian parsley

*P*repare the cucumbers as described on page 88.

With a vegetable peeler, remove the zest from 1 lime very carefully, taking as little white pith as possible. Cut the peel into very fine strips until you have about ½ teaspoon. Soften both limes by rolling them on a table, between your palms; they will release their juice more easily this way. Squeeze out the juice; you should have at least 2 tablespoons.

Toss the cucumbers and lime juice together with the remaining ingredients except the salt and parsley. Refrigerate, covered, for at least 30 minutes. Before serving, remove the garlic and add the salt and parsley.

Life-span: 3 hours, well covered, in the refrigerator

Marinated Mushrooms
4 servings

1	pound white mushrooms
1	green bell pepper, roasted (page 88) or 1 raw red pepper, seeded and cut into julienne strips
5	medium whole scallions, cut into thin rounds
4–6	large fresh basil leaves, minced, or 1 teaspoon dry basil
1	heaping tablespoon chopped Italian parsley
1	garlic clove, finely minced
2	tablespoons red-wine vinegar
2	tablespoons tarragon vinegar
1	tablespoon sherry vinegar
⅓	cup soy oil
½	cup fruity olive oil
½	rounded teaspoon salt
¼	teaspoon freshly ground pepper

Wipe the mushrooms clean with a cloth napkin. Trim off approximately ¼ inch on each stem. Place in a flat-bottomed glass, stainless-steel, or plastic bowl, add the remaining ingredients, and toss gently to coat the mushrooms. Leave at room temperature for 1 hour, gently tossing the mushrooms with the marinade at 15-minute intervals. Refrigerate and marinate overnight. Serve cold or at room temperature. Check seasonings before serving.

Life-span: 2 days, well covered, in the refrigerator

Wild Mushroom Salad

6 servings

*T*his is an extravagant salad. If you want to splurge, you won't be disappointed. We recommend using fresh *shiitake* mushrooms for two reasons: First, they are the only "wild" fresh mushrooms in commercial distribution. Second, their subtle, woodsy flavor and meaty texture can improve any recipe requiring fresh mushrooms. Although dried wild mushrooms are available, they are not a good choice for this recipe because they become too spongy once they have been reconstituted by soaking.

1½	pounds fresh *shiitake* mushrooms, sliced
¼	cup hazelnut or walnut oil
¼	cup light virgin olive oil
4	teaspoons freshly squeezed lemon juice
½	teaspoon salt
⅓	teaspoon freshly ground black pepper
1	tablespoon minced fresh chives

Cut any dried ends off the mushrooms, wipe or wash the mushrooms, and pat dry carefully. Cut into ⅛–¼-inch slices. The mushrooms will be cooked in four batches. Place a 9-inch sauté pan over high heat and add ⅛ cup of both the nut and olive oil. When the oil is hot, add ¼ of the mushrooms; they should just cover the bottom of the pan so that they can brown quickly without stewing. Stir them often to coat with oil, reduce the heat to medium, and sauté until slightly brown. Move mushrooms to one side of the pan, tilt the pan, and press excess oil from the mushrooms. Remove them with a slotted spoon and transfer to a medium-size bowl. Sprinkle and toss each batch of mushrooms with 1 teaspoon of lemon juice. Raise the heat and sauté the second batch in the oil remaining in the pan. Use the remaining ¼ cup of combined oils for remaining batches. Toss the mushrooms with the salt, pepper, and chives. Serve warm or at room temperature. The delicate flavor of this salad is masked by refrigeration.

Life-span: 2–3 hours at room temperature, if tossed periodically

Egg Salad
6 servings

12   extra-large Hard-cooked Eggs (page 35), still
      slightly warm, peeled and cut in ½-inch
      pieces

1   cup plain yogurt

¾   cup ricotta cheese

½   cup finely chopped scallions

2   tablespoons sesame seeds, lightly toasted in a
      frying pan over medium heat

1   teaspoon caraway seeds

1   tablespoon poppy seeds

¼   teaspoon freshly ground black pepper

1   teaspoon salt

*I*n a medium-size bowl, combine thoroughly all the ingredients, except the eggs. Stir the warm egg pieces into the mixture. Serve
immediately or chill.

Life-span: 48 hours, well covered, in the refrigerator

Tortellini Vinaigrette
with Ham and Vegetables
4–6 servings

1   pound frozen *tortellini*

     Salt for water

1   tablespoon olive oil

¼   pound prosciutto, thinly sliced and cut into
      julienne strips

1   teaspoon soy oil

¼   pound Black Forest ham, thinly sliced and
    cut into julienne strips

2   small red bell peppers, roasted (page 88) and
    cut into julienne strips

1   cup blanched asparagus tips and stems, cut
    into thin rounds *or* broccoli broken into
    small flowerets and blanched

⅓   cup thinly sliced scallions, white parts and
    ⅓ of green tops

1   recipe Vinaigrette (page 76)

½   teaspoon salt or to taste

⅓   teaspoon of freshly ground pepper or to taste

¼   cup freshly grated Parmesan cheese

*G*ently separate any *tortellini* that may be stuck together. In a large kettle, bring 4–6 quarts of water to a boil and add 1 teaspoon salt per quart of water and the olive oil. Drop the *tortellini* into the boiling water a few at a time, allowing the water to come back to the boil after each addition. Also, from time to time, stir with a wooden spoon to prevent the pasta from sticking. Cooking time is about 4–5 minutes. When the *tortellini* are done but still firm, turn them out into a colander and run cold water over them for a couple of minutes to cool and stop the cooking. Drain and set aside.

In a small sauté pan, sauté the prosciutto with the teaspoon of soy oil until crisp. Drain on a paper towel.

In a mixing bowl, combine the *tortellini* and all the remaining ingredients except the Parmesan cheese and prosciutto. Toss well together. If serving immediately, also sprinkle in the cheese. (Do not refrigerate with the cheese as it has a tendency to coagulate the vinaigrette.) Garnish the salad by crumbling the prosciutto over each portion. Serve immediately.

Life-span: 6 hours, well covered, in the refrigerator

Tortellini with Pesto Mayonnaise
4–6 servings

1   pound frozen *tortellini*

Salt for water

1   tablespoon olive oil

Pesto Mayonnaise

2   medium cloves garlic or 2 teaspoons Roasted
Garlic purée (page 81)

2   tablespoons pine nuts

1   cup basil leaves, loosely packed

2   tablespoons tarragon vinegar

1   extra-large whole egg

1   extra-large egg yolk

1   teaspoon Dijon mustard

1   teaspoon salt

¼   teaspoon freshly ground black pepper

2   tablespoons olive oil

¾   cup soy oil

⅓   cup minced raw carrot

1   tablespoon minced fresh chives

Food processor or *blender*

Cook the *tortellini* as in the preceding recipe. Set aside in a medium-size bowl.

Purée the garlic and pine nuts in the food processor or blender. Stop the motor. With a rubber spatula scrape down the sides of the container. Add all the remaining ingredients, except the oil, carrot, and chives. Make the mayonnaise as directed on page 76.

Combine the *tortellini*, the pesto mayonnaise, and the minced carrot and chives. Toss together and serve. This salad can be refrigerated but is best eaten immediately. (The mayonnaise gets gummy if the salad is held too long.)

Life-span: 6 hours, well covered, in the refrigerator

Capellini Salad with Chèvre Dressing
4–6 servings

½   pound *capellini*

1   tablespoon olive oil

½   cup soy oil

2   tablespoons olive oil

1½ teaspoons salt

½   teaspoon freshly ground pepper

1   tablespoon minced fresh chives

1   tablespoon chopped parsley

3   tablespoons chopped fresh dill *or* basil

1   red bell pepper, roasted (page 88) and minced

Chèvre Dressing

½   cup heavy cream

¼   cup *chèvre* (goat) cheese

1   tablespoon tarragon vinegar

1½ teaspoons Dijon mustard

¼   teaspoon salt

⅛   teaspoon freshly ground pepper

1½ teaspoons freshly squeezed lemon juice

Food processor

*P*urée all the ingredients for the dressing in the food processor until they form a smooth paste.

In a kettle, bring 2 gallons of water with 1 tablespoon of salt to a boil. Add the 1 tablespoon of olive oil and *capellini* and bring back to the boil. Cook for 3½ minutes, immediately turn out into a colander, and run under cold water to stop the cooking. Place the *capellini* in a large bowl and mix them thoroughly with the oils to prevent clumping. Then mix in the salt, pepper, herbs, roasted pepper, and *chèvre* dressing. This salad is best served immediately, as the pasta will clump together after a short time in the refrigerator.

Life-span: 1 hour at room temperature

Curried Rice Salad
8 servings

1½ cups long-grain white rice

3 cups White Stock (page 116) *or* water

1½ teaspoons salt

½ cup julienne strips of carrot

½ cup julienne strips of white part of leek

1 teaspoon medium-hot curry powder

¼ teaspoon ground cumin

¼ teaspoon minced garlic

2 heaping tablespoons grated red radishes

2 tablespoons pine nuts, toasted in a preheated 350°F. oven for 5–10 minutes, or until golden

2 tablespoons freshly squeezed lime juice

1 tablespoon red-wine vinegar

2 tablespoons soy oil

1 tablespoon chopped parsley

1 teaspoon minced fresh dill

2 tablespoons thinly sliced scallion

2 heaping tablespoons chutney

*I*n a kettle, bring the stock to a boil, add the rice and the salt, stir, and reduce to a simmer. Cook for 20–25 minutes, until rice is tender but still firm. Drain in a sieve and rinse under cool water to stop the cooking. (An alternative method is to remove the rice from the heat a few minutes before it is done and to allow it to drain in the sieve without rinsing. The rice will continue to cook in its own heat for a few minutes and more of the stock flavor will be retained.) When drained well, place the rice in a mixing bowl.

Combine all the remaining ingredients and add to the rice. Toss well and serve warm or slightly chilled. (If chilled, remove from the refrigerator 1 hour before serving.)

Life-span: 6 hours, well covered, in the refrigerator

Carrots with Rosemary, Salmon Galantine, Marinated Beets,
Broccoli with Garlic Mayonnaise, Marinated Mushrooms

Above: Tenderloin of Beef with Poached Eggs and Beurre Rouge

Right: Sole Stuffed with Lobster Mousse with Red Pepper Sauce Vivarois

Crudités and Hors d'Oeuvre with Chinese string beans

Above: French Toast

Left: Pâté de Campagne, Calf's Liver Pâté, Duck Pâté

Liz Sanchez's Meringue Chocolate Chip Cookies and Gingersnaps with Fresh Ginger, Meringue Pineapple, Very Rich Chocolate Cake with Chocolate Curls, Papaya Tart, Wild Rice Pudding in orange shells, Watermelon Sorbet

Wild Rice Salad

8 servings

3   cups cool cooked wild rice

1   small Granny Smith apple, peeled and coarsely chopped

¼   cup peeled and finely minced Granny Smith apple

⅓   cup currants

½   cup walnuts (see NOTE), toasted in a preheated 350°F. oven for 5–10 minutes, or until golden

¼   cup red-wine vinegar

2   tablespoons walnut oil

⅓   cup olive oil

*I*n a large mixing bowl, combine all the ingredients. Using a fork, make certain that the minced apple is thoroughly incorporated as it has a tendency to clump.

This salad should be served immediately. It can only be out at room temperature on a cool day for about 1 hour. It can be refrigerated for a few hours. However, as refrigeration tends to harden the grains of rice and ruin the texture of the salad, we suggest taking it out 1 hour before serving.

Life-span: 6 hours, well covered, in the refrigerator

NOTE: Chopped hazelnuts, pecans, almonds, macadamia nuts, or Brazil nuts can also be toasted and used in this salad.

New Potato Salad

8–10 servings

3	pounds red new potatoes, washed (see NOTE)
6½	teaspoons salt, in all
¾	teaspoon freshly ground black pepper
1½	tablespoons sherry vinegar
2	tablespoons tarragon vinegar
¼	cup dry white wine or vermouth
⅓	cup fruity olive oil
2	tablespoons soy or walnut oil
1	tablespoon minced shallots
⅓	cup coarsely chopped scallions, white and green parts
⅓	cup loosely packed chopped herbs (dill, parsley, tarragon)

*I*n a large saucepan, cover the potatoes with about 4 quarts water, add 4 teaspoons salt, and bring the water to a boil. Lower the flame so that the potatoes cook at a medium simmer until they are easily pierced with a fork, approximately 20 minutes. Drain and rinse briefly under cool water for 1 minute. While the potatoes are still warm, cut them into thirds and add the remaining ingredients except the scallions and herbs. It is important to add the dressing while the potatoes are still warm so that the flavors are absorbed. Add the scallions and herbs after the salad has cooled or they will discolor. Serve at room temperature or chilled.

Life-span: 2 days, well covered, in the refrigerator

NOTE: For a part of the new potatoes, you may substitute any of the following: 1 pound rutabaga, cooked, peeled, and cubed; 1 pound turnip, cooked, peeled, and cubed; 1 pound carrots, scraped, cooked, and cut into chunks.

Seafood Salad with Herb Mayonnaise

8 servings

4   cups cooked seafood, chilled

You will need approximately 2¼ pounds boneless fish such as fresh tuna, sea or bay scallops, salmon, or bass fillets, poached, flaked, and chilled. Or use 8–12 pounds mussels, steamed, shelled, and chilled.

Herb Mayonnaise

2   extra-large egg yolks
    Juice of 1 lemon

1   teaspoon tarragon vinegar

2   tablespoons chopped Italian parsley

1   tablespoon plus 1 teaspoon chopped fresh dill

1   teaspoon chopped fresh chives

1   teaspoon salt

¼   teaspoon freshly ground pepper

1   cup soy oil

3   tablespoons *Crème Fraîche* (page 27)

Combine all the ingredients, except the oil and *crème fraîche*. Make the mayonnaise as directed on page 76. Finally, stir in the *crème fraîche*. Gently combine the cooked seafood with the mayonnaise and serve immediately, or chill. All seafood salads should be made the day they are served.

Life-span: 6 hours, well covered, in the refrigerator

Scallops Seviche

4 main course, or *6 appetizer servings*

1½	pounds bay scallops, rinsed and drained
¼	cup fruity olive oil
5	tablespoons tarragon or rice-wine vinegar
1	tablespoon dry white wine or vermouth
¼	cup diced roasted red bell pepper (page 88)
1	tablespoon chopped Italian parsley
½	teaspoon finely minced garlic
2¼	teaspoons salt
¼	teaspoon Tabasco

*I*n a medium-size mixing bowl, combine all the ingredients. This salad can be served immediately or it can be chilled and served after a few hours or the following day. If you do not serve it immediately stir the salad periodically.

Life-span: 24 hours, well covered, in the refrigerator

Shrimp Salad with Red Pepper and Herb Mayonnaise

6–8 servings

3	pounds jumbo shrimp (preferably fewer than 15 shrimp per pound)
6	quarts cold water
2	tablespoons kosher salt
	Small sprig thyme
6	cloves garlic, gently smashed but unpeeled
½	lemon, thinly sliced
1	large or 2 small bay leaves

Red Pepper and Herb Mayonnaise

1 extra-large egg yolk

½ roasted red bell pepper (page 88) or pimiento

2 tablespoons tarragon vinegar

3 medium scallions, white and green parts, chopped

1 tablespoon Dijon mustard

2 teaspoons freshly squeezed lemon juice

   A pinch of cayenne pepper

½ teaspoon salt

1 cup soy oil

1 teaspoon chopped fresh dill

1 teaspoon chopped parsley

2 level teaspoons peeled, seeded, and chopped fresh tomato or 2 canned plum tomatoes

1 heaping tablespoon minced red bell pepper

   Food processor

*F*or the shrimp, combine all ingredients, except the shrimp, in a stainless-steel or enameled kettle, bring the water to a boil, and simmer for 15 minutes. Drop in the shrimp and cook for 2½–4 minutes, depending on their size (the largest shrimp take 4 minutes), until they begin to curve but are not completely curled up. Drain in a colander and plunge immediately into ice water or place under cold running water to stop the cooking. Peel, devein, rinse, and pat dry.

Make the mayonnaise: Place all the ingredients except the oil, herbs, tomatoes, if used, and red pepper in the food processor and purée for 30 seconds. Slowly add the oil, remove mixture to a bowl, and stir in the remaining ingredients by hand. To serve, mix together the shrimp and mayonnaise. Chill before serving.

Life-span: 12 hours, well covered, in the refrigerator

Tuna Curry Salad
4–6 servings

Two 7-ounce cans fancy albacore solid white tuna packed in water or 1 pound poached chilled fresh tuna

½ medium tart green apple, unpeeled and thinly sliced

1 large or 2 small scallions, thinly sliced, white part and ⅓ of green tops used

⅓ cup slivered almonds (see NOTE), toasted in a preheated 350°F. oven for 10–15 minutes

3 heaping tablespoons finely diced celery

1½ teaspoons salt

2 tablespoons currants *(optional)*

*D*rain the canned tuna in a sieve and press out remaining water with your hand or the back of a large spoon. Transfer the tuna to a large bowl, flake it with a fork, and mix in the remaining ingredients. Set aside.

NOTE: Roasted unsalted peanuts may be substituted for the almonds.

Curry Mayonnaise

¼ teaspoon cuminseeds

¼ teaspoon minced garlic

½ teaspoon grated fresh ginger

1 extra-large egg yolk

1½ teaspoons red-wine vinegar

Juice of ½ lemon

½ teaspoon salt

⅛ teaspoon freshly ground pepper

2 teaspoons medium-hot curry powder

2 rounded tablespoons chutney

⅔ cup soy oil

Food processor

First, in a mortar, grind together the cuminseeds, garlic, and ginger. Combine this mixture and all the remaining ingredients, except the oil and chutney, and make the mayonnaise as directed on page 76. Stir in the chutney last.

Assembly

With a fork, mix the salad ingredients and the mayonnaise together thoroughly. The tuna should be well flaked and the whole mixture moistened by the dressing.

Life-span: 24 hours, well covered, in the refrigerator

Chicken with Tarragon Mayonnaise
6 servings

Three   12- to 14-ounce unboned chicken breasts

*P*reheat the oven to 375°F. In a baking pan, roast the chicken breasts for 30–45 minutes. Cool to room temperature. Carefully remove all the meat from the bones, discarding the skin, fat, and tendons. Cut into bite-size pieces, approximately 1-inch cubes. Place the chicken in a mixing bowl and set aside.

Tarragon Mayonnaise

2	extra-large egg yolks
2	tablespoons tarragon vinegar (see NOTE)
2–3	tablespoons chopped tarragon leaves (see NOTE)
2	teaspoons Madagascar green peppercorns packed in brine, drained (see NOTE)
3–4	sprigs parsley (see NOTE)
1	teaspoon salt
¼	teaspoon freshly ground pepper
1	cup soy oil
2	tablespoons heavy cream
1	tablespoon finely chopped shallots
	Food processor

In the food processor, place all the ingredients except the oil, heavy cream, and shallots. Make the mayonnaise as directed on page 76, transfer to a small bowl, and stir in the cream.

Spoon the tarragon mayonnaise over the chicken. Add the shallots and mix thoroughly. Chill for 15 minutes, adjust the seasoning, serve. Or, place the salad in the refrigerator and remove 1 hour before serving.

Life-span: 24 hours, well covered, in the refrigerator

NOTE: You may use only 1 tablespoon tarragon vinegar and 1 rounded table-spoon tarragon leaves packed in vinegar, drained, and lightly squeezed to remove liquid.

When making this mayonnaise by hand, first mash the green peppercorns in a mortar with a pestle and mince the parsley sprigs. (Also chop vinegar-packed tarragon leaves, if used.)

Duck and Orange Salad
8–10 servings

We use mallard or Muscovy ducks. Although they are expensive and difficult to find, their flavor is well worth the trouble of getting them. Fresh Peking ducks are adequate and readily available.

This is a two-day project.

3	ducks, approximately 4–5 pounds each, eviscerated
2	cups Duck Stock (page 117)
½	cup cold water
2	teaspoons gelatin
3	juice oranges
3	tablespoons plus 1 teaspoon sherry vinegar
1	tablespoon honey
1	teaspoon puréed green peppercorns (Madagascar peppercorns preserved in brine, drained, and mashed in a mortar with a pestle)

1   cup walnut pieces

¼   cup walnut oil

2   tablespoons soy oil (for duck cracklings)

1   teaspoon whole green peppercorns preserved in brine, drained

2   dozen snow peas, cut into fine julienne strips

2   dozen green beans, blanched briefly and cut into thin rounds

2   tablespoons chopped scallions

1   tablespoon chopped parsley

2¾   teaspoons salt

¼   teaspoon freshly ground pepper

1   cup cooked wild rice *(optional)*

Preheat oven to 400°F. and roast the ducks for 40–45 minutes, or until they are medium rare. Cool to room temperature. Remove all the skin and as much fat as possible; reserve enough duck skin to total 6–8 inches square. With a long thin-bladed knife, remove each breast in one piece and cut the meat on a diagonal into slices ¼ to ⅓ inch thick and 1½ inches long. Remove the remaining meat, discarding the tendons and remaining fat. Getting the leg meat off the bones is a tedious process, but it is important to persevere and get as much meat as possible, free of fat and tendons. (Keep wiping down the board you are working on, as it tends to become extremely greasy, making it difficult to see what you are doing.) Place all the useable meat on a plate, cover, and refrigerate. This yields about 4½ cups duck meat.

Make the duck stock with the carcasses and all the bones. When the stock has cooled, skim off the fat. Reduce 2 cups of the stock to ¾ cup. Soak the gelatin in the cold water, add this to the hot duck stock, and mix thoroughly to make certain the gelatin is dissolved completely. Transfer to a bowl and refrigerate until firm.

The recipe may be made a day in advance up to this point.

Grate the whole oranges until you have 3 tablespoons of grated rind. Cover and reserve.

Peel the oranges: Place on a cutting board and, with a sharp boning knife, start from the top of the orange and cut just through the skin and white membrane around to the bottom of the orange. Cut off the skin in sections all around the orange. Try to cut away as little of the actual fruit as possible, while still being careful to remove the white membrane completely. Next, hold the peeled orange over a bowl to catch the juice and with your knife cut in on either side of each section to free the fruit from the inner membranes. Place the orange sections in a large mixing bowl and reserve.

Combine the juice that escaped from the oranges (about ½ cup), sherry vinegar, and honey and stir in the green peppercorn purée. Reserve.

Sauté the walnuts in the walnut oil over a medium-low flame until they are golden brown. Reserve.

Cut the piece of reserved duck skin into ½-inch squares and sauté these in the soy oil over a medium flame until they are crisp and golden brown. Drain the cracklings on paper towels and reserve.

Assembly

Remove the duck meat from the refrigerator. Remove the jellied duck stock from its bowl and chop coarsely; refrigerate again.

Combine the duck meat with the reserved orange sections, spicy orange-juice mixture, orange rind, sautéed walnuts, and all the remaining ingredients except the jellied stock and the cracklings. At the last moment, fold in the stock and sprinkle the cracklings on top of the salad. Serve immediately.

Serving suggestions: You may add the optional cup of cooked wild rice to this salad, or, instead, accompany the duck salad by the Wild Rice Salad on page 97. Or serve it with Wild Mushroom Salad, page 91. The duck salad can also be presented in hollowed-out orange shells.

Smoked Turkey Waldorf Salad
4–6 servings

1   pound smoked turkey, skinned, trimmed of any dry edges, and cut into bite-size pieces (approximately 1-inch cubes)

1   medium endive, cut into julienne strips

1   green apple, thinly sliced or diced

¾   cup diced celery

1   cup seedless grapes, halved

1   cup tightly packed watercress leaves

⅓   cup currants soaked in ¼ cup Madeira wine for 30 minutes and drained

⅓   cup walnut or pecan pieces

Mayonnaise

The ¼ cup Madeira used to plump the currants

¼   cup freshly squeezed orange juice

¼   cup applejack

1   extra-large egg yolk

3   tablespoons freshly squeezed lemon juice

1½ tablespoons freshly squeezed orange juice

½   teaspoon salt

¼   teaspoon freshly ground pepper

⅔   cup soy oil

2   tablespoons *Crème Fraîche* (page 27)

Food processor or *blender*

*I*n a small stainless-steel or enameled skillet, over medium heat, reduce the Madeira, orange juice, and applejack to 2 tablespoons, transfer to a small container, and cool. Then place it and all the mayonnaise ingredients, except the oil and *crème fraîche*, in the food processor or blender and make the mayonnaise as directed on page 76. Transfer to a bowl and stir in the *crème fraîche*.

Assembly

Toss all the salad ingredients together in a mixing bowl. Add the mayonnaise and mix gently. Chill for 2 hours or serve immediately.

Life-span: 24 hours, well covered, in the refrigerator

Tenderloin and Calf's Liver Salad

6–8 servings

1   pound tenderloin of beef, tied to insure oval
    shape and even cooking

1   pound calf's liver in one piece, membrane
    and any tubes removed, tied into a tube
    shape and rubbed with 1 tablespoon olive oil

*P*reheat the oven to 400°F. Insert a meat thermometer in one end of the beef tenderloin, place the meat in a small baking pan, and roast it for 35 minutes, or until it reaches medium rare (125°F.). (Less time is required if you use a narrow tail end rather than a center cut.) Remove the tenderloin from the oven and let it rest to redistribute the juices.

Lower the oven temperature to 350°F. Place the liver in another small pan and bake for 20 minutes. Remove the liver and allow it a short resting period of about 20 minutes. Do not refrigerate the liver or beef; it would tend to dull their flavors.

Strain the juices from both pans and reserve. While the meat is resting, prepare the dressing, radishes, and garlic croutons.

Dressing and Radish Garnish

1½   bunches red radishes, grated (approximately
     ¾ cup)

½   cup Vinaigrette (page 76)

¼   teaspoon salt

2   tablespoons of the grated radishes

1   tablespoon minced *cornichons* (sour French
    pickles)

⅛   teaspoon salt

¼   teaspoon cracked black pepper

    The reserved pan juices (see NOTE)

To the ¾ cup grated radishes add 1 tablespoon of the vinaigrette and ¼ teaspoon salt. Set aside. To the vinaigrette add all the remaining ingredients and whisk together well.

Garlic Croutons

2   tablespoons Clarified Butter (page 24)

2   tablespoons olive oil

2   cloves garlic, minced

1   cup diced fresh bread (trim off crust before cutting bread into ¼-inch dice)

⅛   teaspoon salt

In an 8-inch frying pan, over a medium flame, combine the clarified butter and olive oil and heat for about 1 minute. Add the garlic and bread cubes and toss continually until the cubes are golden brown, approximately 1 minute. Remove the croutons from the pan and drain on paper towels. Salt and set aside.

Assembly

Cut the calf's liver and beef tenderloin into thin slices, approximately ¼ inch thick. On a platter or a shallow flat-bottomed serving dish, place a slice of liver, then a slice of beef slightly overlapping it. Continue alternating the slices until you have arranged all the meat on the platter. Between the slices place a small amount of the seasoned grated radish. Pour the dressing over the salad and garnish with the garlic croutons and any grated radish that you may have left over.

Serving suggestions: Cold Capellini Salad (page 95) or New Potato Salad (page 98) are good accompaniments.

Life-span: None; once assembled, the salad must be served immediately.

NOTE: If you double this recipe, do not use more than 3 tablespoons of meat juices in the dressing.

Salade Chinoise I

4 servings

We make two versions of this salad, one a light all-vegetable mixture, the other a substantial salad with strips of marinated roast pork loin.

Dressing

½   teaspoon minced garlic

2   tablespoons rice-wine vinegar

1   tablespoon sherry vinegar

2   tablespoons sesame oil

1   tablespoon *sake*

2   tablespoons soy sauce

¼   teaspoon hot pepper sesame oil *(optional)*

Combine all the dressing ingredients together in a bowl and set aside.

Salad Ingredients

2   tablespoons sesame seeds, toasted for 15 minutes in a preheated 350°F. oven

½   cup (⅛ pound) blanched snow peas, strings removed

1   cup fresh bean sprouts

½   cup sliced water chestnuts

¼   pound bamboo shoots, sliced

½   cup dried Chinese black mushrooms, soaked until softened, squeezed, drained, stemmed, and sliced

1   cup diagonally sliced scallions

¼   cup julienne strips of red bell pepper (about ¼ small pepper) *(optional)*

When you have prepared all the ingredients for the salad, you may cover and refrigerate them, without the dressing, for up to 12 hours. To assemble, toss the salad ingredients so they are evenly distributed, add the dressing, and toss again. Serve as soon as possible.

Life-span: 3 hours after mixing, well covered, in the refrigerator

Salade Chinoise II
4–6 servings

*F*or this version, double the amount of all the ingredients of the dressing in Salade Chinoise I. The salad ingredients remain the same.

*Chinese Roast Pork Lilah Kan

Marinade:

⅔ cup hoisin sauce

⅓ cup tomato catsup

¼ cup packed brown or white sugar

¼ cup soy sauce

¼ cup dry sherry

2 medium-size cloves garlic, peeled and finely minced

1½ pounds boned and trimmed pork loin, cut into strips approximately 5 inches long, 2 inches wide, and 1½ inches thick

Mix the marinade ingredients and marinate the pork strips in it, refrigerated, for 3 hours.

Remove the lower racks of your oven and place one rack at the highest position. Place a shallow roasting pan containing 1 inch of water on the bottom of the oven. Preheat the oven to 325°–350°F.

*From *Introducing Chinese Casserole Cookery*, by Lilah Kan, Workman Publishing, New York, 1978.

Make S-shaped hooks of poultry lacers (very thin, short skewers; in a pinch you can use paper clips). Insert one end of a hook into the top of each pork strip. Using kitchen tongs, hang the hooks from the top rack, making sure all the meat is positioned over the pan of water. (The water catches the drippings and prevents your oven from smoking. It also helps to keep the pork moist and tender.) You must have a 9- or 10-inch clearance from top rack to water or the meat will hang in the water.

Roast the pork for 40–45 minutes. To make sure the pork is cooked through, cut into the center of the thickest piece. If the juices run clear, the pork is done. If the juices are pink, cook all the pieces a little longer. Be careful not to overcook the pork, or it will have a dry, tough texture.

Remove the meat from the oven, again using kitchen tongs, and allow it to cool. When you have prepared the pork and all the ingredients of the salad, you may cover and refrigerate them, *unmixed*, for up to 12 hours.

To assemble the salad: Slice the cooled roast pork into pieces ⅛ inch thick and 1 to 2 inches long and place them in a mixing bowl. Sprinkle the sliced pork with the 2 tablespoons of toasted sesame seeds (see the salad ingredients). Add all the remaining salad ingredients, tossing them lightly so they are evenly distributed. Next add the double recipe of salad dressing and toss the salad again. Serve as soon as possible.

Life-span: 3 hours after mixing, well covered, in the refrigerator

Ham Salad with Artichokes and Almonds

4–6 servings

1¼ pounds Black Forest ham, or other flavorful ham, cut into julienne strips ⅛ × 2 inches

8 large cooked artichoke bottoms, sliced and marinated in a mixture of the juice of 3 lemons, a pinch of salt, 2 tablespoons fruity olive oil, and 1 tablespoon dry white wine

2 tablespoons chopped Italian parsley

¼ teaspoon freshly ground black pepper

2 stalks celery, thinly sliced on the diagonal

2 tablespoons finely chopped scallions

½ cup small cubes Fontina or aged Gouda cheese *(optional)*

½ cup toasted slivered almonds

Rémoulade Sauce

2 extra-large eggs

1 teaspoon mustard

2 tablespoons tarragon vinegar

Juice of ½ orange

1 cup soy oil

½ cup olive oil

1 tablespoon small capers

1 heaping tablespoon minced *cornichons* (sour French pickles)

2 Hard-Cooked Eggs (page 35), finely chopped

½ teaspoon salt

A pinch of freshly ground pepper

*P*repare the rémoulade sauce base with the first six ingredients, using the mayonnaise process (page 76). This dressing in its final stage, however, is thinner than regular mayonnaise. Now add the capers, *cornichons*, and chopped eggs, and season with the salt and pepper. You should have about 2 cups of sauce. Combine all the salad ingredients first, then toss with the rémoulade sauce.

Life-span: 6 hours, well covered, in the refrigerator, reserving almonds and tossing them in just before serving

Soups
&
Sandwiches

*W*ith the exception of the court bouillon, all the stocks in this chapter may be concentrated by gently simmering until only one third of the original amount is left. Then pour into ice-cube trays and freeze. This is rather like preparing your own bouillon cubes: When the stock is needed, water may be added to reconstitute the frozen cubes to the original amount. For a home kitchen this proves very convenient.

STOCKS

White Stock

Makes 4–5 quarts

3   pounds veal bones, cut into 2- to 3-inch pieces (by the butcher)

2   fowl

1   parsnip, peeled

2   onions, halved and stuck with a clove

2   leeks, root ends trimmed, split, and washed

2   stalks celery, halved

4   carrots, halved

1   clove garlic, unpeeled

10 peppercorns

1   bunch parsley stems

    Bouquet Garni

5½ quarts water

    Stockpot

*P*lace the veal bones in the stockpot with cold water to cover, bring to a boil, and simmer for 5 minutes. Drain, rinse the bones, and put them in a stockpot with the remaining ingredients; the water should cover the bones by 1 inch. Bring to a boil, carefully skimming the foam that rises to the surface. When all the foam has been removed, cook the stock at a gentle simmer, uncovered, adding water if necessary and skimming the foam, for 4–5 hours.

Drain and taste the stock. If it is not fully flavored, boil until it is further reduced. Cool the stock, chill it, and remove the fat. The stock will keep, tightly covered, in the refrigerator, 3–4 days. Boil again for 5–10 minutes to keep another 3–4 days, refrigerated. White stock can also be frozen.

Duck Stock
Makes 1–2 quarts

2	oranges, halved
2	pears, halved
2	stalks celery, coarsely chopped
2	carrots, coarsely chopped
1	small onion, coarsely chopped
3–4	duck carcasses (see NOTE)
2–3	parsley stems
1½	teaspoons salt
3	white peppercorns
1	bay leaf
1	teaspoon thyme
¾	teaspoon sage
	Stockpot

*P*reheat the oven to 450°–500°F. In a shallow pan, roast the first five ingredients until they are dark brown in color, approximately 45 minutes. Transfer to the stockpot, add the duck carcasses and all the remaining ingredients, and cover with cold water. Bring to a boil, skim, and simmer for 4 hours, skimming from time to time. Strain the stock through a sieve lined with cheesecloth wrung out in cold water.

NOTE: Recipes that yield 3–4 duck carcasses are Duck and Orange Salad (page 104), Duck Pâté (page 146), and Duck Sausages (page 159).

Fish Stock
Makes 4 quarts or more

*T*his stock freezes well.

3   pounds carcasses of striped bass or sole and trimmings

6   quarts cold water

1   medium carrot, coarsely chopped

2   small leeks, coarsely chopped, white parts only

1   small onion, coarsely chopped

     3-inch piece celery

9   parsley stems

12 peppercorns

6   whole allspice

3   cloves

1   large bay leaf

¼   teaspoon dried thyme leaves

1   cup dry white wine

Remove gills and bloody clots from fish carcasses. Wash carcasses and trimmings well, put into an enameled or stainless-steel kettle, and cover with the cold water. Bring just to a boil, turn heat down immediately to a very slow simmer, and skim off foam as it rises to the surface. When foam stops rising noticeably, add all the other ingredients, except the wine, and simmer for 30 minutes, skimming as necessary. Then add the wine and simmer 20 minutes more. Strain the stock through a sieve lined with cheesecloth. Allow to cool, then refrigerate or freeze.

Tomato-Fish Stock
Makes 1 quart

*T*his delicious stock can be made at your leisure and then frozen. Use it as the basis for a fish stew of your own devising, with the freshest fish and vegetables in the market, or as the broth for a Manhattan clam chowder.

2   pounds white fish heads, bones, and trimmings

2   cups thinly sliced onions

1   cup thinly sliced white of leek

¾   cup olive oil

2   cups dry white wine

6   cups water

3   pounds ripe tomatoes or 5 cups canned tomatoes, coarsely chopped

½   cup coarsely chopped fresh fennel *or* ½ teaspoon fennel seeds, crushed

1   small bay leaf

⅛   teaspoon thyme

6   peppercorns

6   parsley stems

Sauté the fish bones, onions, and leeks in the olive oil over medium-high heat for about 10 minutes. Add the remaining ingredients, bring to a boil, and simmer for 1 hour. Strain the stock, pressing on the fish and vegetables with the back of a spoon to extract as much liquid as possible.

Court Bouillon

Makes 3 cups

5 cups water

Zest of 1 lemon

3 young carrots, thinly sliced

1 medium onion, thinly sliced

1 small leek, thinly sliced

3 star anise

½ teaspoon mashed green peppercorns

6–8 black peppercorns

½ cup dry white wine

Combine all the ingredients, except the wine, in a stainless-steel saucepan or small stockpot, bring to a boil, and simmer over a low flame for 40 minutes. Add the wine and allow to bubble softly for 10 minutes. Strain into a bowl, cool, and refrigerate.

SOUPS

Purée of Acorn Squash Soup
4–6 servings

2 acorn squash, halved and seeded

½ cup coarsely chopped onions

4 tablespoons sweet butter

2 cups White Stock (page 116)

1 quart water

3–4 sprigs fresh thyme or a pinch of dried thyme

A pinch of freshly grated nutmeg

1 teaspoon salt

¼ teaspoon freshly ground black pepper

¼–¾ cup heavy cream

3–4 red radishes, grated

2 tablespoons chopped fresh chives *or* Italian parsley

Food processor, blender, or *food mill*

*P*reheat the oven to 350°F. Place the acorn squash, cut side down, on a lightly buttered baking sheet and bake until tender, 35–40 minutes, being careful not to brown or burn them. When fork-tender, remove from the oven and turn them cut side up to cool.

In a 2½-quart saucepan, over medium-low heat, lightly sauté the onions in the butter until translucent, about 8–10 minutes. When squash is cool, scoop out the flesh, being careful not to take any skin. Measure about 3 cups of squash and add to onions with the stock, water, thyme, nutmeg, salt, and pepper. Simmer, uncovered, for 15–20 minutes. Pass through a sieve set over a bowl to catch the liquids. Purée the solids in the food processor, blender, or with a food mill, adding some of the liquid to facilitate the process. Return purée and liquid to the saucepan, bring to a simmer, and taste for seasoning.

To serve, ladle soup into warm bowls, add 1–2 tablespoons of heavy cream to each bowl to make a creamy mass in the center, sprinkle with the radishes, and top with a large pinch of chopped chives or parsley. Serve very hot.

Sugar Snap Pea Soup with Mint

6 servings

1	pound sugar snap peas, ends snapped off and strings removed
1	cup chopped onions
3	tablespoons sweet butter
1½	quarts White Stock (page 116)
2	cups water
8	fresh mint leaves
	Kosher salt to taste
	A large pinch of black pepper
	Food processor or *blender*

*I*n a 4-quart pot, over low heat, slowly cook the onions in the butter until translucent but not brown. Stir in the stock and water and simmer, uncovered, for 10 minutes. Add the sugar snap peas and blanch for 1–2 minutes. Pour the mixture through a sieve set over a large bowl to catch the liquid. Purée the solids in the food processor or blender with some of the liquid, about ¼ cup liquid to 2 cups peas and onions. It is a good idea to purée in batches for a consistent texture, adding the mint leaves to the last batch. Blend the purée and reserved liquid and add salt and pepper to taste. Serve immediately.

Leek and Bell Pepper Soup

6–8 servings

¼   pound Westphalian ham, in all, diced

¼   cup fruity olive oil

1   cup finely chopped yellow onions

1½   cups sliced white of leeks

2   medium cloves garlic, thinly sliced

2   cups red and/or green bell peppers, cut lengthwise into ¼-inch strips, then cut in half

2   medium bay leaves

     A large pinch of saffron threads

1   small sprig fresh thyme or ½ teaspoon dried thyme

1   level tablespoon kosher salt

2   quarts White Stock (page 116) *or* Duck Stock (page 117)

½   cup dry white wine

*I*n a 3½- to 4-quart kettle, over medium heat, sauté 2 ounces of the ham in the olive oil for 5 minutes. Add the onions, leeks, garlic, and peppers and cook for 10 minutes. Add the bay leaves, saffron, thyme, salt, stock, and wine, bring to a simmer, and cook, uncovered, for 25–30 minutes. While the soup is cooking, fry the remaining ham crisp in a little oil, crumble it, and reserve for garnish. Serve in heated soup bowls; sprinkle each serving with the crumbled ham.

NOTE: If you feel ambitious one day when you're preparing this soup for special friends, while the soup simmers, sauté croutons and grate fresh Parmesan cheese to add to each bowl just before serving. This hearty peasant soup can also be made with any leftover ham or hambone.

Cucumber-Yogurt Soup
6–8 servings

6–7	medium cucumbers, peeled
3½	cups plain yogurt
¾	cup heavy cream
1¾	cups White Stock (page 116)
1½	teaspoons chopped fresh dill
½	teaspoon freshly ground white pepper
½	teaspoon kosher salt
1	teaspoon minced fresh chives
⅛	teaspoon cayenne pepper
1	teaspoon freshly squeezed lemon juice
1	tablespoon minced red onion *(optional)*
2	tablespoons chopped Italian parsley
8–10	lemon wedges
	Food processor or *blender*

Slice the cucumbers in half lengthwise, with a teaspoon, scoop out all the seeds and discard. Cut the cucumber into chunks and purée in the food processor or blender. Press the purée through a medium-fine mesh sieve into a large bowl, whisk in the yogurt, the cream, and stock. Add the next 7 ingredients and whisk lightly. Chill and serve garnished with the parsley and lemon wedges.

Sarah's Navy Bean Soup with Smoked Beef

6–8 servings

1   cup dried navy beans, washed, soaked for 3–4 hours, and drained

2   small onions, coarsely chopped

2   stalks celery, coarsely chopped

2   parsnips, peeled and coarsely chopped

½   pound fatty salt pork or pork rinds, cut into small strips

½   cup chopped Italian parsley

6   tablespoons sweet butter

2   quarts boiling water *or* White Stock (page 116)

2   bay leaves

    Salt to taste

¼   teaspoon freshly ground pepper

1   cup chopped smoked beef *or* smoked ham

    Food processor, blender, or food mill with medium blade

Sauté onions, celery, parsnips, salt pork, and parsley in the butter. Add water or stock, bay leaves, salt, and pepper and bring to a boil. Add drained beans and simmer for 1 hour. Add the smoked beef and cook 30 minutes, or until the beans are tender. Discard bay leaves. Purée soup in the food processor or blender or put through the medium blade of a food mill. Serve hot.

Fennel Consommé

4–6 servings

3	fennel bulbs, root ends removed and coarsely chopped
1	onion, finely chopped
1	small celery root, peeled and diced
½	cup dry white wine
1	bay leaf
1	teaspoon salt
¼	teaspoon freshly ground white pepper
1	star anise
½	cup Pernod or Ricard
2	quarts cold White Stock (page 116)
2–3	extra-large egg whites
1	cup very finely chopped chicken breast (fat and skin removed)
½	cup julienne strips of fennel
2	tablespoons finely chopped fennel tops

*I*n a 4- to 6-quart saucepan, steam the fennel, onion, and celery root in the wine, covered, for 5–10 minutes. Add the bay leaf, salt, pepper, and star anise, cover, and simmer over low heat for 5 minutes. Add the Pernod, cover, and simmer 10 minutes more. Add the cold stock and remove from heat.

To clarify the stock, whisk the egg whites and chopped chicken into the soup, which should be just warm to the touch. (If it is too hot, the egg whites will coagulate before they can mix with the impurities in the stock.) Place the pot over medium heat and *do not disturb*. After 10 minutes, pieces of egg white will make their way to the surface of the stock and eventually form a "raft" to cover the whole surface. The stock should *not* boil at any time, but should simmer gently once the egg whites start to rise to the surface. In 15 minutes, when most of the egg whites have surfaced, turn off the heat, let the mixture sit for a few minutes, and then carefully remove enough of the raft so that you can get a small ladle into the clear stock beneath it. Gently, so as not to break up the raft unduly, draw out the stock, ladle by ladle, and pour it through a few thicknesses of damp cheesecloth into a tureen. Adjust the seasoning with salt and white pepper, if needed. To serve, garnish with the julienne of fennel and fennel tops.

Garlic Soup

6–8 servings

1½	large heads of garlic, broken into separate cloves, unpeeled
2	cups boiling water (for blanching the garlic)
3	small sprigs fresh thyme or ½ teaspoon dried thyme
2–3	leaves fresh sage or ⅛ teaspoon crumbled dried sage
4	cloves
1	large bay leaf
2½	quarts water
1	tablespoon kosher salt
¼	teaspoon freshly ground black pepper
¼	cup fruity olive oil
½	cup chopped cooked fresh spinach

"Mayonnaise" Liaison

3	extra-large egg yolks, at room temperature
¼	cup olive oil

Optional Garnishes

1	cup cooked egg pastina
½	cup sautéed chopped fresh spinach
¼	cup freshly grated Parmesan or Romano cheese

Food processor or *blender*

*P*lace garlic cloves in the 2 cups boiling water for 30 seconds, drain, and place under cold running water. (This assures easy peeling and removes the acrid taste.) Peel the garlic and place it with all the other soup ingredients in a 4-quart saucepan. Bring to a boil and maintain a fast simmer for 30 minutes.

While the soup is cooking, prepare the liaison: Beat the yolks until pale and sticky; then, drop by drop, beat in the oil until well combined. Set aside.

When the soup has finished cooking, strain it through a sieve into a bowl. Remove the bay leaf and cloves from the sieve, and purée the solid ingredients with 1 cup of broth in the food processor or blender. Return the purée and the remaining broth to the saucepan. Adjust the salt and pepper to taste, remembering that the grated cheese added at the end is also salty. Briskly whisk together the egg yolks and olive oil liaison, then whisk this into the hot broth just before serving, making certain that the soup does not boil again, which would cause the mayonnaise to curdle. Serve the soup in heated bowls, adding to each a small scoop of pastina and a big pinch of spinach, if desired, and a generous sprinkling of grated cheese.

Jerusalem Artichoke Soup
6–8 servings

*J*erusalem artichokes are also known as *topinambour,* but they are usually labeled sunchokes when packaged. They are the root of a variety of sunflower and can be eaten raw, sliced into a salad, or used in much the same way as the potato. Their distinct flavor mingles well with garlic and lemon—thus the idea for this soup.

1½	pounds unpeeled Jerusalem artichokes, thinly sliced (see NOTE)
	Juice of 2 lemons
¼	pound (1 stick) sweet butter
2	cups packed sliced yellow onions
1½	teaspoons minced garlic
1	tablespoon freshly squeezed lemon juice

1½ teaspoons kosher salt

⅛ teaspoon freshly ground pepper

2½ quarts White Stock (page 116)

¼ cup thinly sliced scallions

¼ cup diced red bell pepper

¼ teaspoon minced fresh thyme or a small pinch of dried thyme

1 cup heavy cream *(optional)*

2 chopped Jerusalem artichokes *(optional)*

3 tablespoons chopped Italian parsley *(optional)*

Food mill with medium blade

To prevent discoloration, keep the sliced Jerusalem artichokes in a bowl of water to which the juice of 2 lemons has been added.

In a 4- to 6-quart saucepan (preferably one that is shallow and wide, rather than deep), over a low flame, melt the butter. Add the artichokes and sauté until they begin to soften, about 15 minutes. Add the onions, garlic, the 1 tablespoon lemon juice, salt, and pepper and continue to sauté until the onions become translucent and the artichokes are quite soft. Turn up the heat, add the stock, and bring to a boil. Boil, uncovered, for 10 minutes, reduce the heat, and simmer for 30 minutes more. Five minutes before the soup is done, add the scallions, red pepper, and thyme. Put the soup through a food mill using the medium blade. This will result in a fairly smooth textured golden soup with flecks of red and green. Add the cream and heat the soup, but do not let it boil. Garnish with the chopped Jerusalem artichokes and parsley. Serve at once.

NOTE: If you prefer a perfectly smooth texture, you can purée the soup in several batches in a food processor. In this case, the Jerusalem artichokes must be peeled, no easy task as they are quite small and quite knobby.

Cream of Celery Root Soup

6–8 servings

5	medium celery roots
2–3	cups water mixed with the juice of 2 lemons
1½	medium yellow onions, finely chopped
4	tablespoons sweet butter
1	large baking potato
1½	quarts White Stock (page 116)
2	cups water
1	tablespoon kosher salt
½–¾	teaspoon freshly ground pepper
½	cup heavy cream
3	tablespoons chopped Italian parsley
	Food processor or *blender*

*I*n a 4- to 6-quart kettle, over medium-low heat, cook the onions slowly in the butter until soft and translucent, about 12–15 minutes.

While the onions are cooking, peel and slice the celery roots ¼ inch thick and drop the slices immediately into the water and lemon juice mixture to prevent discoloration. Peel and slice the potato and submerge with the celery root. When the onions are soft, drain the celery root and potato and stir them into the onions. Cook for about 2 minutes, then add the stock, water, salt, and pepper (always start with a smaller amount of seasoning and adjust it later). Bring to a boil, lower the heat, and simmer, uncovered, for about 35 minutes, or until the vegetables are tender.

Remove the soup from the heat, allow it to cool slightly, then pour it into a sieve over a bowl, reserving the broth. In the food processor or blender purée the solids with about 2 cups of the broth, then stir the purée back into the remaining broth.

When ready to serve, bring the soup to boiling point and add the cream. Immediately turn off the heat, check the seasonings, and serve sprinkled with the parsley.

Tomato-Orange Soup
6–8 servings

2½   pounds fresh or canned plum tomatoes

6   juicy medium navel oranges

¼   pound (1 stick) sweet butter

1½   cups thinly sliced onions

1   star anise

2   teaspoons kosher salt

1   bay leaf

Grated rind of 1 medium orange and
½ lemon

½   cup dry white wine (preferably Muscadet or
Sancerre)

5   cups White Stock (page 116)

1   cup *Crème Fraîche* (page 27) *or* sour cream

¼   cup chopped fresh basil

Food mill with medium blade

*R*emove the stem end and any green flesh from the fresh tomatoes and cut into sixths. Grate the rind of 1 orange and reserve. With a small sharp knife, remove the rind and white pith from all the oranges, cutting close to the flesh. Holding the oranges over a bowl, cut them into sections by slicing between the pulp and the membrane; discard the cores. Reserve the flesh and the juice.

In an enameled or stainless-steel kettle, melt the butter over a low flame, and sauté the onions slowly. As they release their liquid and begin to soften, add one third each of the oranges and tomatoes. Simmer slowly for 10–15 minutes. As the liquid evaporates, add the star anise, salt, bay leaf, grated rinds, and white wine. Then add the remaining tomatoes and oranges and the stock, bring to a boil, reduce the heat to medium, and let the soup simmer slowly for 5–10 minutes more. Remove the bay leaf and star anise. Press the soup through a medium sieve or put through the medium blade of a food mill. This soup is best served immediately while still hot; or cold, with a dollop of *crème fraîche* or sour cream and chopped basil.

Scallop and Oyster Bisque
4–6 servings

1	white of leek, coarsely chopped
1½	cups coarsely chopped carrots
2	cups coarsely chopped onions
1	quart Fish Stock (page 118)
2	cups water
1	clove garlic, smashed and peeled
10	whole black peppercorns
2	bay leaves
½	teaspoon fennel seeds
½	teaspoon curry powder
1	cup dry white wine
1	pound sea scallops, rinsed and sliced ¼ inch thick
1	endive, cut into julienne strips
2	cups heavy cream
2	cups milk
1	teaspoon salt
8–12	fresh oysters, shucked
	A pinch of chopped fresh chives for each bowl of soup
	A pinch of good quality paprika for each bowl of soup

*I*n a 6-quart pot, combine the leek, carrots, onions, stock, water, garlic, peppercorns, bay leaves, fennel seeds, and curry powder and simmer, uncovered, for 15 minutes. Add the wine and simmer for another 5 minutes. Remove the pot from the heat, strain, reserving the broth and discarding the solids. Wash the pot, return the broth to it, and, at a very low simmer, poach the scallops in it for approximately 30 seconds, or until they are just done. Remove the scallops with a slotted spoon and set them aside in a sieve over a bowl. Pour back into the soup any liquid released from the scallops and, over medium heat, reduce the broth to 3 cups. Add the endive and simmer for 2–3 minutes. Then add the cream, milk, and salt and heat. Add the scallops and oysters and heat them for only about 30 seconds, or until the edges of the oysters curl. Serve the soup immediately in hot bowls. Garnish each bowl with the chopped chives and a dusting of paprika.

Pear Soup with Fresh Ginger

4–6 servings

2¾	pounds ripe Bartlett or Anjou pears
¼	pound (1 stick) sweet butter
2	cups thinly sliced onions
2	level teaspoons finely minced fresh ginger, or 1½ teaspoons ground ginger
2	teaspoons kosher salt
1	tablespoon freshly squeezed lemon juice
5	cups White Stock (page 116)
¼	teaspoon freshly ground white pepper
1	tablespoon chopped Italian parsley, *or* fresh mint

Food processor, blender, or food mill

*P*eel, halve, core, and slice the pears. Melt the butter in an 8-quart stockpot. Add the onions and soften over a low flame. Add the pears and stir frequently over a low flame until they nearly "melt" and the onions become translucent.

Add 1 teaspoon of the ginger, the salt, and lemon juice. Add the stock and bring to a boil. Add remaining ginger (if you are using ground ginger, taste to see if the soup is already pungent enough) and pepper; simmer for 10–15 minutes. Purée in the food processor or blender, or put through food mill. This soup has an ethereal quality when it is just done, and it is best served immediately. Garnish with the parsley or heady fresh mint leaves.

Kale Soup with Fennel Meatballs
6–8 servings

¾ cup thinly sliced onions

½ cup thinly sliced carrots

2 cloves garlic, thinly sliced

3 tablespoons olive oil

3 cups firmly packed kale leaves, torn from the stems and roughly chopped

1 quart water

1 quart fresh White Stock (page 116)

1 tablespoon kosher salt

¼ teaspoon freshly ground black pepper

Meatballs

6 ounces lean veal

6 ounces lean pork

½ cup minced onion

2 tablespoons sweet butter

2 tablespoons chopped Italian parsley

2 teaspoons fennel seeds, 1 teaspoon crushed in a mortar

½ teaspoon hot pepper flakes

1 teaspoon kosher salt

1 egg

2 tablespoons bread crumbs

*I*n a 2½-quart saucepan, over medium-low heat, cook the onions, carrots, and garlic in the oil until the onions are translucent but not colored, about 8–10 minutes. Add the kale and stir until it is a deep lustrous green, about 3 minutes. Add water, stock, salt, and pepper and bring to a boil. Lower the heat to a simmer and cook, covered, for 20 minutes.

Grind the veal and pork together twice, or have your butcher do it. Cook the onion in butter over low heat until it is translucent, about 8 minutes, then cool it. Stir the onion and the remaining ingredients into the ground meat and mix until well combined. Form miniature meatballs, using about 1 heaping teaspoon of the mixture for each. Ten minutes before serving, drop the meatballs into the simmering soup and cook until they are firm to the touch, about 8–9 minutes. Ladle soup into heated bowls and divide the meatballs among them.

SANDWICHES

Gorgonzola Cheese and Salami Sandwich

2 servings

2–3	thin slices yellow onion
2	teaspoons olive oil
	8-inch piece crusty French or Italian bread, split in half lengthwise
1	tablespoon plus 1 teaspoon crumbled Gorgonzola cheese crushed with 2 teaspoons cream cheese
¼	pound Genoa salami, thinly sliced

*O*ver a low flame, sauté the onion slices in the oil for 2–3 minutes, until tender and slightly brown. Remove the pan from the heat and set aside. Spread each slice of bread with 1 tablespoon of the cheese mixture. Place the salami and the onions on one of the bread halves and top the sandwich with the other bread half. Cut the sandwich in half and serve immediately.

Serving suggestion: Marinated Mushrooms (page 90)

The six sandwiches that follow are among the most popular at The Soho Charcuterie. Several of them are filled with salads found earlier in the book, and all of them are so easy to assemble that we have listed only the ingredients.

Tuna Curry on Black Bread
1 serving

⅔   cup Tuna Curry Salad (page 102)

2   thin slices black or whole-grain bread

Serving suggestion: Corn Salad II (page 87)

Black Forest Ham and Brie
1 serving

2   ounces ripe Brie, rind removed

2   ounces Black Forest ham, thinly sliced

8–10   inches crusty French bread, split in half
lengthwise

Serving suggestion: Carrots with Rosemary (page 82)

Charcuterie Hero
1 serving

5   thin slices capicolla

2   thin slices prosciutto

4   thin slices Genoa salami

2   thin slices fresh or smoked mozzarella

3   thin slices red onion

3   thin slices red bell pepper

¼   pimiento, cut into strips

8–10   inches crusty Italian or French bread, split
in half lengthwise

Sprinkle with

Coarsely ground pepper

Salt

Red-wine vinegar

Olive oil

Serving suggestion: Marinated Beets (page 79) and sour pickles

Shrimp Salad on Black Bread
1 serving

5   large shrimp from Shrimp Salad with Red Pepper and Herb Mayonnaise (page 100)

¼   ripe avocado, thinly sliced *(optional)*

2–3   sprigs watercress

2   thin slices black bread

Serving suggestion: New Potato Salad (page 98)

Chicken Tarragon in Brioche
1 serving

¾   cup Chicken with Tarragon Mayonnaise (page 103)

1   individual brioche, hollowed out

Garnish

Avocado slices

Watercress sprigs

Charcuterie Club
1 serving

½   cup Chicken with Tarragon Mayonnaise (page 103)

2   slices bacon, fried until crisp and drained

¼   ripe avocado, thinly sliced

2   thin slices black or whole-grain bread

Serving suggestion: Grated Salad I (page 83)

Smoked Salmon and Asparagus Sandwich
1 serving

1   ounce smoked salmon, thinly sliced

2   spears asparagus, blanched and cut into julienne strips

1   scallion, root and green tips trimmed

Pinch salt

1   teaspoon *Crème Fraîche* (page 27) *or* sour cream

1   teaspoon *chèvre* (goat) cheese

1   thin slice rye or black bread, crusts removed

*P*reheat the oven to 500°F. In a small saucepan, poach the scallion in simmering water with a pinch of salt for 10 minutes, or until it is tender. Remove the scallion from the water with a slotted spoon, pat it dry, and set aside. Mix the *crème fraîche* and the *chèvre* together and spread on the bread. Place on a baking sheet and bake for 2–3 minutes. Transfer to a plate, place the smoked salmon on the cheese, then arrange the asparagus over the salmon. Drape the scallion so that part of it lies on the sandwich and part on the plate. Serve immediately.

Serving suggestion: Cucumber Salad with Lime (page 89)

Vegetarian Hero

2 servings

8–10	inches French or Italian bread, split in half lengthwise
⅓	pound ripe Brie, rind removed
¼	ripe avocado, thinly sliced
8–10	paper-thin slices peeled cucumber
2	diced marinated mushrooms (see NOTE)
8–10	julienne strips of red bell pepper
1	large radish, thinly sliced
1	tablespoon Vinaigrette with chopped fresh dill (page 76) *or* olive oil and red-wine vinegar
2–3	sprigs watercress
¼	cup alfalfa sprouts

Spread each slice of bread with Brie. Next, layer the slices with the avocado, cucumber, mushrooms, red pepper, and radish. Drizzle the vinaigrette over the top of each half and garnish with watercress and alfalfa sprouts. Serve immediately.

NOTE: You can mince the mushrooms and season them with a little vinaigrette. We use Marinated Mushrooms, page 90.

Cold American Hero
or Chef Salad Sandwich
2 servings

8–10 inches crusty French or Italian bread, split
     in half lengthwise

3 tablespoons Vinaigrette (page 76)

2 thin slices roast beef

2 thin slices smoked turkey or smoked
   chicken breast

2 thin slices Black Forest ham

2 thin slices Swiss cheese

3–4 leaves endive, cut into julienne strips

Drizzle each bread half with 1½ tablespoons vinaigrette,
arrange all the remaining ingredients on one of the bread halves, and top with
the other half. Cut into 4 pieces. Serve immediately.

Serving suggestion: Broccoli with Garlic Mayonnaise (page 80)

Cheeseburgers
2 servings

4 slices black or whole-wheat bread, trimmed
  of crust

2 tablespoons plus 1 teaspoon sweet butter,
  in all

½ cup julienne strips of leek

½ pound ground chuck

  Salt and freshly ground black pepper to taste

1 very thin slice Westphalian or other well-
  seasoned ham

2 very thin slices Swiss or Fontina cheese

*P*reheat the oven to 500°F. Melt 1 tablespoon of the butter, brush the bread with it, and toast in the oven for about 5 minutes. Heat the broiler. In the meantime, over a low heat, sauté the leeks in 1 teaspoon of the butter for 1–2 minutes. Remove the pan from the heat and set aside. Next, season the meat with salt and pepper and shape it into 2 round patties approximately the size of the bread. In the remaining tablespoon of butter, over a low flame, fry the hamburgers to the desired degree of doneness, and arrange the leek, ham, and cheese on top. Cover the pan briefly to melt the cheese, transfer the cheeseburgers to 2 slices of bread, and cover with the remaining slices. Serve immediately.

Serving suggestion: Potatoes Sautéed with Duck Fat and Cracklings (page 163) and sour pickles

Tuna Melt Sandwich
2 servings

10	inches crusty French or Italian bread, split in half lengthwise
2	tablespoons olive oil
3½	ounces canned tuna fish, drained
2	anchovy fillets, finely minced
1	teaspoon finely chopped celery
1	teaspoon capers, drained
½	teaspoon minced onion
1	teaspoon minced red bell pepper
½	teaspoon finely minced garlic
1	tablespoon grated Swiss cheese
½	teaspoon freshly squeezed lemon juice
	Salt and freshly ground pepper to taste

Topping

6   julienne strips of red bell pepper

2   anchovy fillets *(optional)*

2   tablespoons grated Swiss cheese

---

*P*reheat the oven to 500°F. On a baking sheet, brush the bread halves with olive oil and toast them in the oven for 5 minutes, or until lightly browned. Leave the oven on. In a small bowl, combine the remaining ingredients. Divide the mixture in half and generously mound on the bread. Top each half with the red pepper strips and an anchovy, if desired, and sprinkle the top with the grated cheese. Bake the sandwich for 5–10 minutes, or until the cheese has completely melted. Serve immediately.

Serving suggestion: Summer tomatoes or mixed green salad with herbed Vinaigrette (page 76)

Reuben Sandwich

2 servings

1   green apple, peeled, cored, and finely grated

¾   cup finely grated green or red cabbage

4   tablespoons sweet butter at room temperature

      A splash of Calvados

      A splash of red-wine vinegar

1   teaspoon caraway seeds

      Salt and pepper to taste

2   slices dark pumpernickel or rye bread

2   thin slices Swiss cheese

4–5   thin slices Black Forest or Smithfield ham, briefly sautéed in 1 tablespoon sweet butter

*S*queeze the grated apple fairly dry in a cloth. Sauté the apple and cabbage in 1 tablespoon of the butter over medium heat for 5 minutes, or until most of the juices have evaporated. Add the Calvados, vinegar, caraway seeds, and salt and pepper to taste. Remove the pan from the heat and set aside. On 1 slice of bread, place a slice of cheese, a couple of slices of ham, followed by the cabbage-apple mixture, then the remaining ham and cheese. Top with the other piece of bread. Spread each side of the sandwich with 1½ tablespoons softened butter. Fry the sandwich in a sauté pan over a medium heat until the cheese has melted, approximately 5 minutes. Flip the sandwich over with a spatula and fry the other side. This sumptuous sandwich should be eaten immediately.

Serving suggestion: Sour pickles

Toasted Sandwiches

1–2 servings

8–10   inches French or Italian bread, split in half lengthwise

1   Filling Recipe (below)

Topping

¼   cup grated Swiss cheese

1   tablespoon grated Cheddar cheese

1   teaspoon grated Parmesan cheese

2   teaspoons dark beer

2   teaspoons beaten egg

1   teaspoon flour

½   teaspoon brandy

  A dash of Tabasco

  A pinch of salt

*P*reheat the oven to 500°F. Toast the bread in the oven for 5–10 minutes, or until it is golden brown. Leave the oven on. Prepare the filling of your choice. Combine all the topping ingredients in a small bowl. Place the filling on the bread, cover it with the topping, and bake for 5–10

minutes, or until the cheese is completely melted and has begun to bubble and brown slightly. Serve at once.

Spinach Filling

1½   cups raw spinach

2   teaspoons sweet butter

¼   cup coarsely chopped pimiento or Roasted
     Red Peppers (page 88)

     Salt and pepper to taste

Sauté the spinach briefly in the butter until it is just wilted. Chop the spinach, add salt and pepper to taste, and mix in the pimiento.

Vegetable Filling

¾   cup coarsely chopped mixed vegetables,
     blanched

2   teaspoons sweet butter

     Salt and pepper to taste

Sauté the vegetables in butter until they are tender, then season with salt and pepper. (Carrots, mushrooms, asparagus, cauliflower, and broccoli are good choices.) If you have leftover cooked vegetables, just warm them briefly in the butter.

Chicken Filling

¾   cup sliced cooked chicken

2   teaspoons sweet butter

     Salt and pepper to taste

Ham Filling

¾   cup diced ham (preferably Black Forest
     ham)

2   teaspoons sweet butter

     Salt and pepper to taste

Sauté the ham or chicken briefly in the butter. Season to taste.

Charcuterie

POULTRY & MEAT PÂTÉS

Duck Pâté
16–20 slices

6   mallard or Muscovy ducks or 5 Long Island (Peking) ducks (see NOTE)

1   cup Cointreau or other orange-flavored liqueur

Diced Mixture

1¼   pound marinated duck meat, cut into ¼-inch dice

¼   pound duck liver, cut into ¼-inch dice

¼   pound Black Forest ham, cut into ¼-inch dice

½   pound fresh or salt pork fat, rinsed in cold water and cut into ¼-inch dice

2½   tablespoons finely minced scallions or shallots

1   extra-large egg white

1½   teaspoons salt

1   teaspoon dried thyme

1   teaspoon freshly ground pepper

½   teaspoon ground allspice

2   tablespoons Cointreau or other orange-flavored liqueur (from the marinade)

Ground Mixture

2½   pound marinated duck meat, cut into 1-inch cubes

½   pound veal, cut into 1-inch cubes

½   pound lean pork, cut into 1-inch cubes

1¼   pounds bacon, preservative-free if possible, rind trimmed and cut into 1-inch pieces

3   extra-large eggs

¼   cup chopped Italian parsley

1   tablespoon Cointreau or other orange-flavored liqueur (from the marinade)

1   tablespoon salt

4   medium cloves garlic, finely minced

1½   teaspoons dried thyme

1½   teaspoons ground allspice

1½   teaspoons freshly ground pepper

½   teaspoon ground cloves

1½   pounds salt fatback, rinsed in cold water and thinly sliced

---

Optional

½   cup dried apricots

½   cup shelled unsalted pistachio nuts

2   tablespoons blanched strips of orange peel

Meat grinder or *food processor*

11-cup heavy loaf pan (6-cup loaf pan for half recipe)

Spot-check thermometer

Preparing the Duck Meat

*T*hree to seven days before making the *pâté*, bone the ducks, reserving the livers for the final preparation and the carcasses for Duck Stock (page 117). The skin and fat can be frozen and used later for Potatoes

Sautéed in Duck Fat with Cracklings (page 163). Place the duck meat in a bowl, add the Cointreau, and mix well. Cover tightly with foil or plastic wrap and refrigerate, turning the pieces once a day. When you are ready to make the *pâté*, drain the duck meat and reserve 3 tablespoons of Cointreau for later use. Weigh out 1¼ pounds of duck meat and set it aside with the duck livers for the diced mixture. The remaining duck meat should weigh approximately 2½ pounds or enough for the ground mixture. (A few ounces either way will not adversely affect the finished *pâté*. See NOTE.)

Preparing the Diced and Ground Mixtures

Combine all the ingredients for the diced mixture in a bowl and set aside.

For the ground mixture, grind the duck meat, veal, pork, and bacon to a medium-coarse texture. Place in a large mixing bowl, add the remaining ingredients, and mix well.

Assembling and Baking the Pâté

Preheat the oven to 250°F. Heat a large kettle of water. Line the loaf pan with slightly overlapping slices of fatback, allowing some of it to hang over the sides of the pan. Make certain that the fatback completely covers inside of the pan.

Divide ground mixture into thirds and the diced mixture in half. Place one third of the ground mixture in the pan and press firmly to spread evenly and eliminate any air pockets. Carefully place a tight row of apricots down the center of the ground mixture and sprinkle 2 tablespoons of pistachios and 1½ teaspoons orange peel on each side. Next, press half of the diced mixture evenly over the apricots and nuts. Repeat this process once, then finish with a final layer of ground mixture. Bring up the strips of fatback to cover the top of the *pâté* evenly and tightly. Fit two layers of aluminum foil snugly over the top, crimping the foil around the edge of the pan.

Place the *pâté* in a larger pan, put it in the oven, and pour enough simmering water into the outer pan to come halfway up the sides of the mold. Bake for about 3 hours, or until the internal temperature is 125°–130°F.

When the *pâté* is done, remove it from the boiling-water bath. The loaf must now be weighted for 4 hours in order to press out excess fat and compress the *pâté* so it will slice evenly. Place another loaf pan (or a board of suitable size) on top of the *pâté* and put two bricks or an equivalent weight of heavy canned goods in the pan or on top of the board. Let cool, remove the weights, and refrigerate overnight.

To unmold the *pâté*, carefully run a knife around the inside of the mold, pressing against its sides to avoid cutting the *pâté*. This will create an air pocket to break the vacuum between the mold and the *pâté*. Bang the *pâté* mold on all sides to loosen the loaf so it will slide out more easily.

Remove the *pâté* from the refrigerator 30 minutes before serving. To serve, remove excess fat, leaving a thin layer surrounding the meat. Cut into slices approximately ¼ inch thick. The flavor of the *pâté* improves with time. Carefully stored, it can be used for up to 2 weeks.

Serve with *cornichons* (sour French pickles) and warm toast or crusty French bread.

Life-span: 2 weeks, well covered, in the refrigerator

NOTE: We prefer Muscovy or mallard ducks for flavor. However, they are expensive and may be difficult to find, and in that case fresh Long Island (Peking) duck is acceptable.

If you do not have a scale for weighing the duck meat, divide it into three equal parts. Use one part for the diced mixture and two parts for the ground mixture.

If a smaller *pâté* is more practical for you, reduce the ingredients by half and use a 6-cup mold.

Calf's Liver or Chicken Liver Pâté
16–20 slices

*F*or a smaller loaf yielding 8–10 slices, use half the ingredients and a 6-cup mold.

2¾	pounds calf's liver or chicken livers, membrane and fat removed (approximately 3 pounds before cleaning)
1¼	pounds salt pork fat, rind removed, rinsed in cold water
6	tablespoons sweet butter at room temperature
8	extra-large egg yolks
¾	cup heavy cream
2	tablespoons flour mixed with ⅔ cup brandy
2½	tablespoons dried tarragon or ¼ cup fresh tarragon leaves
1	teaspoon grated fresh ginger
1	tablespoon salt
1½	teaspoons freshly ground black pepper
2	tablespoons green peppercorns, drained *(optional)*
¾	cup pitted diced Niçoise black olives *(optional)*

Meat grinder

Food processor

Fine-mesh strainer

11-cup heavy loaf pan

Heavy baking sheet

Spot-check thermometer

Preheat the oven to 300°F. Using the medium-coarse blade of a meat grinder, grind the liver and pork fat. Next, place half the ground meats and half the butter in the food processor with 4 of the egg yolks and process until the mixture is completely smooth. Transfer to a large mixing bowl and repeat the process. Pass the mixture through the fine-mesh strainer to remove the small pieces of fatback and membrane. Add all the remaining ingredients, making certain not to add the olives and peppercorns until you are ready to transfer the *pâté* to its mold, as they may sink to the bottom. Pour the *pâté* mixture into the mold and place it, uncovered, on a baking sheet on the middle rack of your oven. Bake for approximately 1½ hours, or until the internal temperature is 135°F. Allow the *pâté* to cool, then refrigerate overnight. For unmolding and serving instructions see Duck Pâté (page 149).

This *pâté* has a very smooth and spreadable texture, making it an ideal choice for a party hors d'oeuvre.

Life-span: 1 week, well covered, in the refrigerator

Pâté de Campagne with Green Peppercorns
15–20 slices

1¼	pounds lean pork shoulder, trimmed of fat and muscle and cut into 1-inch cubes
¾	pound lean veal, trimmed of fat and muscle and cut into 1-inch cubes
1	pound fresh pork fat, trimmed of rind and cut into 1-inch cubes
⅓	pound ham, not too bland or too strong (we recommend Black Forest), cut into 1-inch cubes
¼	pound chicken or duck livers
1	small yellow onion
	A 1¾-ounce jar or can of Madagascar green peppercorns, drained
1	tablespoon peppercorn liquid
4	medium cloves garlic, peeled and crushed or finely chopped
2	extra-large eggs, lightly beaten
1½	teaspoons fresh thyme or ½ teaspoon dried thyme
1	tablespoon fresh sage leaves or ⅓ teaspoon dry sage
1½	teaspoons ground allspice
2	juniper berries, crushed *(optional)*
1	tablespoon salt
1½	teaspoons freshly ground pepper
⅔	cup brandy
1	large piece of caul fat *(optional)*
½–¾	pound pork fatback, very thinly sliced
	Meat grinder or food processor
	11-cup heavy loaf pan
	Spot-check thermometer

*G*rind the pork, veal, pork fat, ham, livers, and onion to a medium-coarse texture and place in a large mixing bowl. In the food processor, blender, or with a mortar and pestle, purée half of the can of green peppercorns with the 1 tablespoon of liquid. Add to the ground meat the garlic, eggs, herbs and spices, brandy, puréed green peppercorns, and whole green peppercorns and mix well.

Preheat the oven to 250°F. Heat a large kettle of water.

Line the loaf pan with the caul fat. Over the caul fat, place slightly overlapping slices of fatback, allowing some fatback to hang over on all sides. Make certain that the fatback completely covers the inside of the pan.

Place about one third of the *pâté* mixture in the loaf pan and press it firmly to spread it evenly and eliminate any air pockets. Repeat this process until you have used up the ground mixture. Bring the overlapping strips of pork fat over the top of the ground meat to cover the *pâté* evenly and tightly. Fit two layers of aluminum foil snugly over the top, crimping the foil around the edge of the pan.

Place the *pâté* in a larger pan, put it in the oven, and pour enough simmering water into the outer pan to come halfway up the sides of the mold. Bake for about 2 hours, or until the internal temperature is 135°–140°F.

When the *pâté* is done, remove it from the boiling-water bath. The loaf must now be weighted for 4 hours in order to press out excess fat and compress the *pâté* so it will slice evenly. Place another loaf pan (or a board of suitable size) on top of the *pâté* and put two bricks or an equivalent weight of heavy canned goods in the pan or on top of the board. Let cool, remove the weights, and refrigerate for 1–2 days.

For unmolding and serving instructions see Duck Pâté (page 149).

Life-span: 2 weeks, well covered, in the refrigerator

SAUSAGES

How to Prepare Sausages

Preparation of Hog Casings

*H*og casings can be purchased from your butcher, or ordered from a butcher's supply house (consult your classified directory). The casings are sold by the hank (16–18 casings, each about 20 feet long), or by the yard. If you have never made sausages before, it is probably more practical to buy the casings by the yard. For the recipes in this book, you will need at least 13 feet of casings. Prepare them as soon as possible after purchase.

Rinse the hog casings under cold running water; handle them gently as the casings tend to be fragile.

Insert two fingers into one end of the casing to separate the sides. Attach the open end to the nozzle of the faucet and allow cold water to penetrate the length of the casing. If the casing has an inner membrane, remove it. Place the rinsed casings on damp paper towels until ready to stuff.

Rinse any unused casings, pack them in coarse salt, and store them in the refrigerator if you plan to use them within a month or so, or they may be stored in your freezer indefinitely. If you are keeping them in your refrigerator, sprinkle them with table salt from time to time to keep them at peak quality.

Filling the Casings

To fill the casings, you will need either a 12- to 14-inch pastry bag and two nozzles, each 2 inches long and ½ inch wide at the narrow opening; or a funnel with a ½-inch nozzle and a separate 2-inch-long nozzle. A pastry bag is preferable because it is easier to manipulate.

Cut the casings into 1-foot lengths. Insert one nozzle into the end of a casing. Attach the second nozzle to the pastry bag and fill the bag with the sausage mixture. Squeeze the mixure down to the tip of the bag to make it firm enough to prevent the formation of air pockets in the sausage. Be careful to hold the casing with its nozzle firmly over the nozzle of the bag with one hand while squeezing and twisting the bag with the other hand. Fill each casing segment with about 4½ inches of meat, pushing it far enough into the casing to leave 3–4 inches of empty casing at either end. If the meat cannot be pushed to within 3–4 inches of the end of a casing without tearing it, squeeze 4½ inches of meat into the casing, remove the casing from the nozzle, and, with your fingers, push the meat far enough in to allow about 2 inches of empty casing at the end.

Grasp the empty casing on either side of the sausage and twirl it rapidly, creating little twists at either end with which to tie off the sausage. Trim the ends, making certain not to cut too close to the knots. Each sausage should be about 4–6 × 1 inches.

Storing the Sausages

Wrap the uncooked sausages tightly in plastic wrap and refrigerate for 3 days, at the longest, or freeze.

Spicy Country Sausages

12 sausages

1¼	pounds lean pork
½	pound beef kidney suet
3	medium cloves garlic, finely chopped
¼	cup finely chopped yellow onion
1	small red or green bell pepper, finely chopped
2	tablespoons applejack
1	teaspoon ground dry chili peppers
¼	cup red-wine or cider vinegar
1	tablespoon salt
1	teaspoon cracked black peppercorns
1	teaspoon ground coriander
1	teaspoon ground cumin
1	fresh hot chili pepper, seeded and minced
13	feet hog casings, prepared for filling (see *preceding recipe*)
6	tablespoons sweet butter or Clarified Butter (page 24)
	12- to 14-inch pastry bag with two 2-inch nozzles

*F*inely chop the pork and kidney suet by hand into pieces ⅛ inch or smaller (see NOTE). In a bowl, combine meat mixture with the remaining ingredients and blend well. Fill the casings as described on page 155.

Heat the butter in a frying pan large enough to hold the sausages in one layer. Prick the sausages a few times with a toothpick, place in the pan, and simmer slowly for 15–20 minutes, turning a few times to brown on all sides. If you prefer to bake the sausages, preheat the oven to 375°F., place the sausages in a baking dish, and roast for about 20 minutes. Drain the sausages on paper towels and serve immediately.

NOTE: We have tried machine grinding but find that the sausage has a mealy, dry texture. Hand chopping is time-consuming, but the resulting texture is worth the effort.

Country Sausages
12 sausages

1   pound lean pork

½   pound salt pork fat, rinsed in cold water

1   teaspoon salt

½   teaspoon freshly ground black pepper

½   teaspoon fresh sage leaves or ¼ teaspoon powdered sage

1   tablespoon finely chopped fresh chives

1   tablespoon coarsely chopped Italian parsley

½   teaspoon crushed anise seeds

13   feet hog casings, prepared for filling (page 154)

6   tablespoons sweet butter or Clarified Butter (page 24)

12- to 14-inch pastry bag with two 2-inch nozzles

*F*inely chop the pork and pork fat by hand into pieces ⅛ inch or smaller (see NOTE, above). Combine remaining ingredients, except the casings and the butter, and blend well. Fill the casings as described on page 155 and cook as directed on page 156.

Boudin Blanc

12 sausages

½	pound boned chicken breast, skin, fat, and tendons removed
½	pound lean veal, trimmed of membranes and cartilage
1	pound fresh pork fat
¾	pound yellow onions
½	cup heavy cream
¾	cup fine fresh bread crumbs
3	extra-large eggs
1	teaspoon salt
1	teaspoon freshly ground white pepper
1	teaspoon ground allspice
13	feet hog casings, prepared for filling (page 154)
¼	cup Clarified Butter (page 24)
½	cup dry vermouth

Meat grinder with fine blade

Cut the chicken breast, veal, and pork fat into 1-inch chunks and set aside.

Chop the onions into small chunks, reserve 2 chunks, and put the rest through the meat grinder. Eliminate as much liquid as possible from the ground onions by squeezing them in a cloth or pressing them in a sieve.

Next, put the meats through the grinder twice. After the second time, put the 2 reserved chunks of onion through the grinder to force out the rest of the meat; stop grinding when onion juice starts to appear.

In a small saucepan, bring the cream to a low simmer, remove from heat, and stir in the bread crumbs. Beat the eggs with the salt, pepper, and allspice. Place the bread-crumb-cream mixture, ground meat, onions, and eggs in a large bowl and mix well with your hands to incorporate everything thoroughly.

Refrigerate while you prepare the hog casings for filling (page 154). Chilling the sausage mixture will make it easier to fill the casings as the mixture is much easier to work with when it is cold. Fill the casings as described on page 155.

Cooking the Boudins

Bring the clarified butter and vermouth to a simmer in a pan large enough to hold the *boudins* in one layer. Prick the *boudins* with a toothpick, place them in the pan, and simmer for 15–20 minutes. Do not allow the sausages to boil or they will burst their casings. Drain off most of the poaching liquid and brown the *boudins*.

Duck Sausages
About 12 sausages

*T*his recipe can be prepared in two days. On the first, bone the ducks, render the fat, and make the duck stock. On the second day, make the sausages and cook them. Leftover stock and as many sausages as you wish can be frozen.

4	Muscovy duck breasts, skinned and boned, or 1½ pounds duck meat (the breast and thigh meat from three 4-pound ducks)
¾	pound fresh pork fat
6	tablespoons rendered duck fat, cooled and hardened
1	pound pork shoulder, fat removed
2	tablespoons Duck Stock (reduced from ½ cup of stock, page 117)
5	tablespoons chopped Italian parsley
1½	tablespoons chopped fresh chives
½	cup robust red wine
4	medium cloves garlic, finely minced
1	teaspoon freshly ground pepper
2	teaspoons salt
1	teaspoon fresh thyme or ½ teaspoon dried thyme

½ teaspoon sage

¼ cup chopped unsalted pistachio nuts

2 extra-large eggs

13 feet hog casings, prepared for filling (page 154)

¼ cup Clarified Butter (page 24)

½ cup dry vermouth

By hand mince the duck meat, pork fat, rendered duck fat, and pork shoulder into ⅛-inch pieces. Next, in a medium-size mixing bowl, thoroughly combine the meat with all the remaining ingredients except the butter and vermouth.

Fill the casings as described on page 155.

Cooking the Sausages

Bring the clarified butter and vermouth to a simmer in a pan large enough to hold the sausages in one layer. Prick the sausages with a toothpick, place them in the pan, and simmer slowly, turning a few times, for about 15 minutes. Place the sausages in a 450°F. preheated oven for 10 minutes to brown. (Do not broil.)

Seafood Sausages with Spinach and Watercress

12 sausages

½ pound bay scallops

¼ pound fillet of striped bass

2 extra-large egg whites

¾ cup heavy cream, in all

¼ teaspoon salt, plus 1 small pinch

⅛ teaspoon freshly ground white pepper, plus 1 small pinch

3 grates nutmeg

½   teaspoon grated lemon rind

¼   cup dry vermouth

1   tablespoon *Crème Fraîche* (page 27)

1   cup coarsely chopped raw spinach

½   cup coarsely chopped watercress leaves

1   tablespoon sweet butter

1   ounce fresh salmon, cut into ¼-inch dice

1   teaspoon chopped fresh chives
    Food processor

12   *pieces plastic wrap, 12 × 17 inches*

Cut 6–8 scallops into small dice and reserve. Cut the bass into 1-inch chunks and purée them and the remaining scallops in the food processor for 2 minutes. With the motor running, add the egg whites, ¼ cup of the heavy cream, ¼ teaspoon salt, ⅛ teaspoon pepper, nutmeg, lemon rind, and vermouth and process for 2–3 minutes. Remove the mixture to a mixing bowl, add the *crème fraîche*, and refrigerate the purée.

In the meantime, wilt the spinach and watercress in the butter with a pinch of salt and pepper. Transfer this mixture to a strainer and, with the back of a spoon, press out the excess liquid. Stir into the fish purée the spinach, watercress, diced salmon, diced scallops, and chives. Whip the remaining ½ cup heavy cream and fold it into the mixture. Refrigerate until ready to assemble the sausages.

Assembling and Cooking the Sausages

Follow the instructions for Seafood Sausages for Gumbo (page 190), using 3 tablespoons of mousse for each sausage and poaching for 20 minutes.

Serving suggestion: Serve warm with Vermouth Cream Sauce (page 61).

Life-span: 2 days, well covered, in the refrigerator

The two recipes that follow make splendid accompaniments to our sausages. Warm New Potato Salad (page 98), *cornichons* and mustard, and buttered cabbage with caraway seeds are also delicious served with the sausages.

Carrot-Potato Cakes

5 servings

1	cup grated carrots, squeezed dry
2¼	cups peeled and grated Maine potatoes or other mealy potatoes, squeezed dry (grate just before using to prevent discoloring)
5	tablespoons sweet butter
1	tablespoon finely minced prosciutto
2	teaspoons salt, in all
½	teaspoon freshly ground black pepper, in all
2½	tablespoons chopped fresh chives
2	extra-large egg whites
5	tablespoons plus 2 teaspoons Clarified Butter (page 24)
1	tablespoon rendered bacon fat

*I*n a small frying pan, over a low flame, melt 2 teaspoons of the butter, add the prosciutto, and fry slowly until it becomes opaque and very crisp; watch carefully to prevent burning. Remove with a slotted spoon to drain on paper towels. In the same frying pan, melt 2 tablespoons of the butter, add the grated carrots, and cook, stirring frequently, until they begin to soften but not to brown. Season with ½ teaspoon of the salt and ¼ teaspoon of the pepper, transfer the carrots to a small mixing bowl, and stir in the prosciutto and chives. Set aside.

Season the potatoes with the remaining salt and pepper and stir in the egg whites. Place 2 tablespoons of the grated potato mixture in the palm of one hand, using the other hand to flatten and shape the mixture into the disk. Form 1 tablespoon of grated carrot mixture into a smaller flattened disk and press it on the potato disk. Using a spatula, transfer the pancake to the work table, carrot side up. Carefully spread 2 more tablespoons of the potato mixture over the carrots and press the edges to seal.

Divide the clarified butter and bacon fat between two frying pans and place over medium-low heat. With the spatula, carefully slide the potato cakes into the frying pans, each of which should be large enough to contain four pancakes. After approximately 3 minutes, gently lift the potato cakes to see if they are golden brown. Turn the cakes over carefully and brown the other sides. Drain on paper towels. Serve at once or keep in a 300°F. oven, until ready to serve. Do not reheat.

Potatoes Sautéed in Duck Fat with Cracklings

4–6 servings

½   pound duck fat (see NOTE)

¼   pound duck skin (see NOTE)

1½   pounds new long white potatoes

1   teaspoon salt

¼   teaspoon freshly ground black pepper

2   cloves garlic, minced

Coarsely chop the duck fat and cut the duck skin into ½-inch squares. Place the fat and skins in a heavy-bottomed frying pan and, over a low flame, slowly render the solid fat. When the pieces of skin become crisp and brown, remove the cracklings with a slotted spoon to drain on paper towels. Reserve.

Meanwhile, peel the potatoes, cut them in half lengthwise, then cut them into ¼-inch slices. Pat dry. Pieces of equal thickness are essential for even cooking.

When the fat is completely rendered, increase the heat and when the fat begins to smoke add the potatoes. As soon as the potatoes begin to color, lower the heat to medium. Sprinkle the potatoes with half the salt and pepper. As the slices begin to brown, turn them over and add the rest of the salt and pepper. When the potatoes are brown and crusty, lower the flame, scatter the garlic and cracklings over them, and toss for 1 minute. Drain and serve.

NOTE: Use the duck skin and fat reserved from Duck Pâté (page 146).

SHELLFISH & FISH

Shrimp Mousse
2–3 main course, or 4–5 appetizer servings

Mousse

1½	pounds shrimp, peeled and deveined
3	extra-large egg whites
2	cups heavy cream
1	tablespoon plus 1 teaspoon chopped parsley
1	level teaspoon chopped fresh dill
1	small shallot, minced
¼	cup dry vermouth
1	teaspoon salt
½	teaspoon freshly ground black pepper
¼	teaspoon freshly grated nutmeg

For the Mold

1	pound spinach leaves, well washed
2–3	tablespoons sweet butter

Design

½	cup mixed diced green beans and asparagus, blanched

Food processor

6-cup mold

Spot-check thermometer

Preparing the Mousse

Rinse and thoroughly dry the shrimp. Place them in the food processor and purée to a paste, about 3 minutes. Add the egg whites, blend thoroughly, and with the motor running, slowly pour in the cream. Process until blended. Finally, add the remaining mousse ingredients and process for about 1 minute; do not overblend. Refrigerate the mousse in the processor container with the cover on, or in a mixing bowl, covered, while you prepare the mold.

Preparing the Mold

Preheat the oven to 325°F. In a large kettle of salted water, wilt the spinach leaves for 15 seconds until they are pliable, but still very bright in color. Rinse the leaves in cold water, spread them on paper towels, and blot off any moisture. Generously grease the mold with the butter, then press the leaves flat on the bottom and sides of the mold, overlapping the leaves and allowing them to hang over on all sides.

Assembling and Baking the Mousse

Heat a large kettle of water. Scoop half the mousse mixture into the lined mold and spread it evenly with a spatula. Next, arrange the green beans and asparagus down the center of the mousse and spread the remaining mousse evenly over the vegetables. Bring the spinach leaves over the top of the mousse to cover it completely.

Cover the mold with a double thickness of buttered aluminum foil and place it in a larger pan. Place the pan in the oven and add enough simmering water to come halfway up the sides of the mold. Bake until the internal temperature is 115°–120°F., or for about 45 minutes. Remove the mold from the boiling-water bath and allow it to cool to room temperature. For best results, refrigerate the mousse overnight with the foil cover still in place.

To Serve

Drain the juices from the mousse. If you are serving the mousse hot, preheat the oven to 400°F. Slice the mousse, place the slices either on a baking sheet brushed with Clarified Butter (page 24) or in a shallow baking dish with a little fish stock or mousse liquid in the bottom, and bake, covered with foil, for 10–15 minutes. Serve with *Beurre Blanc* (page 27).

To serve cold, slice the drained mousse and serve with Red Pepper and Herb Mayonnaise (page 101).

Life-span: 2 days, well covered, in the refrigerator

Scallop Mousse

4–6 main course, or 10 appetizer servings (see NOTE)

Mousse

3   pounds sea scallops

5   extra-large egg whites

1   quart heavy cream

2   teaspoons salt

¾   teaspoon freshly ground pepper

   A pinch of cayenne pepper

4   grates nutmeg

For the Mold

1½   pounds spinach, well washed *(optional)*

3–4   tablespoons sweet butter

Design

A handful of mixed diced and blanched vegetables: green beans, broccoli, asparagus, carrots

Food processor

10-cup ceramic or glass terrine

Spot-check thermometer

*F*ollow the instructions for Shrimp Mousse (page 164), but purée the scallops, egg whites, and cream in three batches, adding the remaining mousse ingredients to the third batch. Mix well in a large bowl and refrigerate while you prepare the mold.

If you are not lining the mold with spinach leaves, simply butter the mold well and spread half the mousse over it in an even layer. Arrange the vegetables so that they will form a decorative pattern when the mousse is sliced, cover with the remaining mousse, and proceed, following the instructions for Shrimp Mousse. Serve hot with Vermouth Cream Sauce (page 61).

Life-span: 2 days, well covered, in the refrigerator

NOTE: This recipe can be reduced by halving the ingredients and baking the mousse in a 6-cup mold.

Saffron-Scented Mussel, Bass, and Scallop Pâté
4–6 main course, or 10–12 appetizer servings

Pâté

24	small mussels, well scrubbed, with beards removed
1	pound fillets of striped bass, skinned and cut into 2-inch chunks
1	pound sea scallops, side muscles removed
2	cups heavy cream, in all
1	teaspoon salt, in all
¾	teaspoon freshly ground pepper
4	extra-large egg whites, stiffly beaten
1	cup Tomato-Fish Stock (page 119)
½	teaspoon Spanish saffron threads

For the Mold

1½	pounds spinach, well washed *(optional)*
3–4	tablespoons sweet butter

Design

½	cup julienne strips of white of leek, blanched for 30 seconds
½	cup diced red bell pepper, blanched for 30 seconds

Food processor

12-inch skillet, with cover

10-cup oblong ceramic or glass terrine

Spot-check thermometer

Preparing the Pâté

Rinse and thoroughly dry the striped bass and scallops. Place the fish in the food processor and purée until completely smooth. With the motor running, slowly add ½ cup of the cream and purée until well blended. Add ½ teaspoon of the salt and the pepper, process briefly, and transfer the purée to a mixing bowl. Lightly whip the remaining 1½ cups cream. Fold the cream and the beaten egg whites into the fish and refrigerate.

In the skillet, bring the stock to a simmer, add the mussels (which should fit in one layer), cover tightly, and poach until the shells just open, about 3 minutes. Remove the mussels from the stock and cool. Strain the stock through two double layers of cheesecloth to remove grit and sand and return to the pan. Remove the mussels from their shells, pull off any beards that are still attached, and rinse each mussel individually to remove sand. Drain, pat dry, and set aside to use for design.

Add the saffron and ½ teaspoon salt to the stock, bring to a simmer, and reduce by half, about 15 minutes. Refrigerate the stock for 15 minutes, then fold it into the chilled fish mousse.

Preparing the Mold

Follow the instructions for Shrimp Mousse (page 165).

Assembling the Pâté

Place one third of the fish mousse in the mold and spread it evenly with a spatula. Arrange half of the mussels over the mousse in a symmetrical pattern, then sprinkle with half the leek and red pepper. Cover with another third of the mousse, arrange on it the remaining mussels and leek and red pepper, and cover with the remaining mousse.

For covering the *pâté* follow the instructions for Shrimp Mousse. Bake 45 minutes–1 hour or until the internal temperature is 115°–120°F.

Serve the *pâté* hot with Oyster Cream Sauce (page 28), or cold with Red Pepper and Herb Mayonnaise (page 101).

Life-span: 2 days, well covered, in the refrigerator

Turban of Sole

6–8 main course servings

1½   pounds fillets of sole

4   tablespoons sweet butter, in all, melted

1   pound spinach leaves, well washed, blanched
     for 15 seconds, and spread on paper towels

Scallop Mousse

1½   pounds sea scallops

3   extra-large egg whites

2   cups heavy cream

¼   teaspoon salt

⅛   teaspoon freshly ground pepper

⅛   teaspoon freshly grated nutmeg

     A pinch of cayenne pepper

Salmon Mousse

¼   pound (after skinning and boning) fresh
     salmon

½   extra-large egg white

     A pinch of salt

     A pinch of freshly ground pepper

     A pinch of freshly grated nutmeg

     A pinch of cayenne pepper

¼   cup heavy cream

Food processor

8-cup Bundt pan or ring mold

Spot-check thermometer

*P*repare the scallop and salmon mousses, following the
directions for Shrimp Mousse, page 164. Refrigerate the mousses for 45 minutes–1 hour to firm them and make them easier to work with.

   In the meantime, gently pound the sole fillets between two pieces of wax paper until they are approximately ¼ inch thick. Brush the mold with 2 table-spoons of the melted butter and line it with the sole fillets, skinned side up so that the white side will show when the dish is unmolded. Overlap the fillets and allow them to extend 1½–2 inches over the sides of the pan. Next, care-fully place 15 or more spinach leaves (depending on the size of the leaves) flat against the sole, completely covering it and extending over the sides of the pan. Refrigerate.

Preheat the oven to 300°F. Heat a kettle of water. With a rubber spatula, gently spread 1 cup of the scallop mousse over the bottom of the mold, tapping the pan against the table to dispel any air pockets and insure an even distribu-tion of mousse. Then wrap the salmon mousse in spinach leaves: On a flat surface, spread out 2–4 spinach leaves (depending on size), place approximately 1½ tablespoons of mousse in the center, and wrap the spinach around the mousse, covering it completely; the package should look like a small cigar. Continue wrapping until you have used up the salmon mousse. Gently press the spinach rolls into the center of the scallop mousse, making certain that they touch end to end, for uniformity of design. Cover with the remaining scallop mousse. Carefully fold the overlapping spinach leaves over to enclose the mousse. Brush the top with 2 tablespoons of melted butter and tightly wrap two layers of foil over the turban. Place the mold in a larger pan, place in the oven, and add enough simmering water to the larger pan to come halfway up the sides of the mold. Bake for about 30 minutes, or until the internal temperature is 115°–120°F. Remove the turban from the boiling-water bath and allow it to rest at room temperature for 2 hours.

To serve hot, preheat the oven to 400°F., return the turban, with its foil cover still in place, to the *bain-marie*, and bake for 15–20 minutes. Drain the liquid from the pan and carefully unmold the turban on a heated serving plate. Serve with Oyster Cream Sauce (page 28).

The turban can also be served cold accompanied by Red Pepper and Herb Mayonnaise (page 101).

Life-span: 2 days, well covered, in the refrigerator

Salmon Galantine
5–6 main course, or 8–10 appetizer servings

Considerable time and care go into the preparation of this dish, but the results are impressive.

2 pounds center-cut salmon, in one piece, skinned and boned

4 quarts Fish Stock (page 118)

Scallop Mousse

¾ pound sea scallops

1 extra-large egg white

¾ teaspoon salt

½ teaspoon freshly ground pepper

¼ teaspoon freshly grated nutmeg

1 cup heavy cream

Design

4 baby Belgian *or* narrow carrots, boiled in salted water for 10–20 minutes and drained

10–12 green beans *or* thin asparagus, blanched in salted water, rinsed in cold water, and trimmed

6 strips salmon, cut ½ inch wide and 4 inches long (about 2 ounces)

1 pound spinach, well washed, blanched for 15 seconds, and spread on paper towels

Heavy knife or *cleaver*

Food processor

Fish poacher

Spot-check thermometer

Carefully remove all small bones from the salmon. Place it between two pieces of wax paper and pound it with the flat side of a cleaver or a meat pounder until it is a rectangle approximately ¼ inch thick, 15 inches long, and 9–10 inches wide. Place the salmon between two wet cloth napkins or double thicknesses of rinsed cheesecloth, place on a baking sheet, and refrigerate 1–1½ hours, allowing it to firm.

Prepare the scallop mousse, following the instructions for Shrimp Mousse (page 164). Refrigerate the mousse for 1–1½ hours. Meanwhile, blanch the carrots and green beans. To prepare the salmon strips for design, wrap each strip in 1–2 blanched spinach leaves and set aside.

Assembling and Baking the Galantine

Place the salmon on your work surface, skinned side down and with the long side parallel to the table edge, and remove the top piece of cloth. Cover the salmon with about 25 spinach leaves, overlapping them slightly. With a spatula, carefully spread half the mousse over the spinach leaves, gently pressing down the leaves if they tend to lift off the salmon. Two inches from the bottom, place 3 wrapped strips of salmon, end to end, in a horizontal row. Repeat for the top side, using the 3 remaining wrapped salmon strips. Next, arrange 3 straight horizontal rows of green beans or asparagus in the center of the rectangle. The rows should be about 1 inch apart and should almost touch the edges of the fish. Lightly cover this first layer of decoration with ½–¾ cup scallop mousse. Using a spatula or your fingers, carefully spread small quantities of mousse over the galantine until only the barest traces of vegetable and salmon can be seen. Down the center, line up the carrots tightly in a single horizontal row, tip to end, and press them gently into the mousse. Cover the carrots with the remaining mousse (about ¼ cup).

To roll and enclose the galantine, follow the basic jelly-roll technique. Lift the napkin from the bottom and very slowly roll and tuck the salmon to the top into a tube shape. Now, wrap the galantine completely in the cloth and tie the roll as you would a sausage or a loin roast, with 18-inch strings approximately 2 inches apart. Gather and tie the cloth tightly at each end.

Bring the stock to a low simmer in the fish poacher or a heavy-bottomed rectangular pan and place the galantine gently in the liquid. Keep the stock at a bare simmer and turn the galantine at 10-minute intervals to insure even cooking. The galantine is cooked when its internal temperature is 110°–115°F., about 30 minutes. Remove from the pan and allow to cool to room temperature. Refrigerate the galantine for at least 8 hours or overnight, so that it will hold its shape when sliced.

The galantine may be served cold with Red Pepper and Herb Mayonnaise (page 101), or it can be reheated. To reheat, preheat the oven to 400°F. Slice the galantine into individual servings, place the slices on either a baking sheet brushed with Clarified Butter (page 24) or in a shallow baking pan with a little fish stock in the bottom, and bake, covered, for 10–15 minutes. Serve with *Beurre Blanc* (page 27).

Life-span: 2 days, well covered, in the refrigerator

Main Courses

Roast Chicken with Garlic, Tarragon, and Crushed Black Peppercorns
4 servings

Four	1¾- to 2-pound young frying chickens (freshly killed if possible)
⅜	pound (1½ sticks) sweet butter, softened
1	teaspoon–1 tablespoon roasted garlic purée (page 81)
8	sprigs fresh tarragon *or* 1 teaspoon minced fresh rosemary
1	tablespoon plus 1 teaspoon crushed black peppercorns
	Sharp boning knife

*I*n a small bowl, mix together 8 tablespoons (1 stick) of the butter, the garlic purée, and tarragon and divide into 4 portions. Gently lift up the skin around the breast cavity of the chickens, leaving a pocket between breast and skin, and spread a portion of the butter-garlic mixture over the breast.

Preheat the oven to 500°F. Place the chickens in a baking pan just large enough to hold them. Smear the remaining butter over the breasts and legs of the birds and sprinkle each with 1 teaspoon of crushed peppercorns. Roast for approximately 20 minutes, or until the legs move easily in their sockets and the skin is quite brown and crisp. Remove from oven and let the birds sit for several minutes. Remove them from the pan, pour off excess fat, and reserve the pan for preparing the sauce.

Sauce

¼	cup tarragon vinegar
⅓	cup dry white wine
1	quart White Stock (page 116)
2	tablespoons heavy cream
1	heaping tablespoon *glace de viande* (optional)

3 tablespoons cold sweet butter, cut into 6–8
   pieces

1 teaspoon chopped Italian parsley

1 teaspoon minced fresh tarragon, rosemary,
   or basil

1 tomato, peeled, seeded, and coarsely chopped

Over a medium flame, deglaze the roasting pan with the vinegar, scraping
up the cracklings and juices with the back of a spatula. When the liquid begins
to bubble, add the wine and bring to a simmer. Strain the liquid into a 12-inch
saucepan, add the stock, and reduce by two thirds. Add the cream and reduce
over medium-high heat for 3–5 minutes. When reduction is the consistency of
honey in a warm room, coating a spoon but not clinging to it, remove the sauce
from the heat, add the *glace de viande*, and incorporate the butter by swirling it,
one piece at a time, into the sauce with a whisk or spoon. Place the pan over a
very low flame from time to time, but do not let the sauce get too hot. Add the
herbs and the chopped tomato. Keep the sauce warm in a *bain-marie*.

Cutting Up the Chickens

Cut up each bird as follows: Place chicken on a cutting board, breast up.
With the tip of a sharp boning knife, nip off and discard the wing tips and turn
the chicken so that its legs point toward you. To remove the legs, insert the
knife between leg and breastbone and slice the skin where the leg meets the
body, then push the leg out and down to expose the hip socket. Carefully insert
knife into the socket and with a strong motion cut the leg from the carcass.
Repeat on the other side. Place the leg, uncut side down, on the board, chop
off the tip of the drumstick of each leg, and discard. To bone and remove the
breasts, turn the chicken so that the neck is facing toward you and, cutting
from the tip of breastbone on one side of the chicken, follow the bone, cutting
down to where the wing meets the carcass. With a sharp cut, sever the wing
joint, leaving it attached to breast. Gently push with your knife from the
breastbone down the sides of carcass and remove breast section; repeat for the
other side.

To Serve

For each serving, arrange 2 legs close together on a heated dinner plate.
Place 2 breast pieces over the legs and pour one fourth of the sauce around the
chicken.

Filets Mignons with
Westphalian Ham and Beurre Rouge
4 servings

Four 6-ounce *filets mignons*, trimmed

¼ cup olive or peanut oil

8 thin slices Westphalian ham

Beurre Rouge

2 tablespoons finely minced shallots

2 cups Cabernet Sauvignon wine

¼ teaspoon salt

1 tablespoon *glace de viande (optional)*

½ pound (2 sticks) sweet butter, cut into ½-inch cubes (leave butter out at room temperature for 30 minutes before using)

⅛ teaspoon freshly ground pepper

Spot-check thermometer

*P*repare *beurre rouge* following the instructions on page 29. Whisk in the *glace de viande* after the wine is reduced and before incorporating the butter. Keep the sauce warm in a *bain-marie* while you prepare the *filets*.

Preheat the oven to 450°F. Heat the oil in a 12-inch sauté pan, over medium-high heat, until very hot; do not allow oil to smoke. Place the beef in the pan and brown on all sides, turning it with kitchen tongs to avoid grease splatters. Remove the *filets* and wrap ham slices around the sides, securing the slices with toothpicks, if they fall off. Place on baking sheet and bake for 10–15 minutes, or until the internal temperature is 120°–125°F. for rare, or 130°F. for medium. The ham will crisp up around the edges. When done, allow the *filets* to sit in a warm place for several minutes before serving.

Spoon 3–4 tablespoons *beurre rouge* onto each serving plate, place the beef on the sauce or to one side of it, and serve immediately.

Herb-Scented Rack of Lamb with Rosé Sauce
4 servings

1   double rack of lamb, cut into four 4-rib
    sections

12 fresh rosemary needles *or* 8 fresh mint
    leaves

4   teaspoons olive oil

2   teaspoons kosher salt

⅛   teaspoon freshly ground pepper

    Spot-check thermometer

Preparing the Rack of Lamb

A double rack of lamb consists of 8 ribs connected to either side of the backbone, a total of 16 ribs. Ask your butcher to trim the rack as follows: Remove the central backbone (chine) from each side of the rack, leaving two 8-rib racks and the backbone. Discard the backbone or freeze and reserve for stock. Cut off about 2 inches from the ends of the ribs and "French" them (use all the trimmings for stock or stew), then evenly trim off some of the fat from the meat side, leaving about a ½-inch layer of fat. Trim off all the fat from the rib (bone) side and cut each rack into 4 ribs.

On the meat side of the sections, using a small pointed knife, make three incisions, 2 inches deep. Insert some of the rosemary into the incisions. Try to embed the herb into the meat so that it does not burn. For each section, rub the outer layer of fat with 1 teaspoon olive oil and sprinkle with ½ teaspoon salt and a few grinds of pepper. The coarse salt not only seasons the lamb, it also helps the fat to crisp during cooking.

Roasting

Preheat the oven to 475°F. Place the lamb on a baking sheet, salted side up, and roast for 15–20 minutes. After 12 minutes, turn the racks over to insure even cooking and continue roasting until cooked to your taste, using the thermometer to show the internal temperature: 125°F. for rare, 130°F. for medium-rare, and 135°F. for medium. Remove the meat from the oven immediately, place on a cutting board, and allow the racks to rest for about 5–10 minutes to reabsorb the juices. While the racks are resting, make the sauce.

Rosé Sauce

1   cup rose wine

2   cups White Stock (page 116) *or* canned chicken stock

4   tablespoons sweet butter, cut into ½-inch pieces

¼   teaspoon kosher salt

⅛   teaspoon very finely chopped fresh rosemary *or* mint

Deglaze the roasting pan with the wine, scraping up all the browned bits of meat with a wooden spoon. Pour the wine into a 12-inch saucepan and reduce by half. Add the stock and, over medium-high heat, reduce to ¾ cup. Over a very low flame, slowly whisk the butter into the liquid, then add the salt (omit salt if you are using canned stock) and rosemary. (The texture of the chopped rosemary should be as fine as sand.)

Slice each rack into 4 chops. Place one fourth of the sauce on each heated serving dish and place the lamb over the sauce. Serve immediately.

Baked Calf's Liver
with Sweet-and-Sour Sauce
6 *servings*

2½–3   pounds calf's liver, in one piece

1   tablespoon olive oil

*P*reheat the oven to 450°F. Place the liver in a shallow baking pan, preferably one that is just large enough to hold it. Rub the liver with the oil. Bake for 12 minutes, then reduce the heat to 275°F. and bake for 15 minutes longer. Turn off the heat and allow the liver to sit in the oven for 10 minutes. Remove from the oven and, with a thin-bladed 12-inch knife, slice the liver thinly. The liver will be pink throughout, with a firm buttery texture. While the liver is baking, prepare the sauce.

Sweet-and-Sour Sauce

4   teaspoons granulated natural cane or brown sugar

2   tablespoons wine or tarragon vinegar

5   cups White Stock (page 116)

5½   tablespoons sweet butter, cut into ½-inch pieces (leave butter at room temperature for 30 minutes)

1   tablespoon freshly squeezed lime juice

½   teaspoon kosher salt

Combine the sugar and vinegar in a 12-inch saucepan or in the top of a 2- to 3-quart double boiler over a medium flame. When the sugar is dissolved, add the stock, bring to a boil, and reduce to 1½ cups. Lower the heat so that the liquid is at a very low simmer and incorporate the butter following the instructions for *Beurre Blanc* (page 27). Add the lime juice and salt. The sauce can be made ahead, kept in a warm place, and reheated.

To Serve

Divide the liver slices among heated dinner plates and spoon the sauce over them. Serve immediately.

Gratin of Scallops
3–4 main course, or *6 appetizer servings*

¾   pound bay scallops, rinsed

1   cup Muscadet or other dry white wine

1   tablespoon minced shallots

1   cup Fish Stock (page 118)

2½   cups heavy cream

1¼   teaspoons kosher salt, in all

2   tablespoons sweet butter

¼   pound *shiitake* or other savory fresh
    mushrooms, trimmed and cut into wedges

½   cup *Crème Fraîche* (page 27)

⅔   large cucumber, peeled, seeded, and cut into
    thin crescents

1   tablespoon freshly squeezed lemon juice

1   teaspoon freshly ground pepper

16   shucked oysters *(optional)*

4   teaspoons fresh bread crumbs

6   *large scallop shells* or *1-quart shallow baking
    dish*

*I*n a 12-inch sauté pan, over a low flame, simmer the wine and shallots until about 2 tablespoons of liquid remain. Add the stock, cream, and ¾ teaspoon salt, and simmer over medium heat until the mixture is reduced by two thirds. Meanwhile, melt the butter in a small sauté pan just large enough to hold the mushrooms and, over high heat, sauté them until lightly golden. Add ½ teaspoon salt, remove from the heat, and set aside. Add the *crème fraîche* and cucumbers to the reduced cream mixture and simmer for a few minutes, swirling the sauce until it is slightly thicker than melted butter. Add the scallops, lemon juice, pepper, and mushrooms and simmer over low heat until the scallops are just barely cooked, about 30 seconds–1 minute. Add the oysters and remove the pan from the heat.

Preheat the broiler. Divide the scallop mixture among the scallop shells or place in the baking dish and sprinkle with the bread crumbs. Slide the shells under the broiler until the tops bubble and brown and an ever-so-thin crust forms on top, only 15–30 seconds, if your broiler is hot enough. Nestle each shell on a bed of kosher salt on an individual serving plate. Serve at once.

Sole Stuffed with Lobster Mousse with Red Pepper Sauce Vivarois
6 servings

This elegant dish is best prepared in stages, beginning with a double recipe of court bouillon. Next, make the lobster mousse, which you can refrigerate while you cook the sauce. Finally, the sole fillets can be filled, placed in their ramekins, and refrigerated until about 45 minutes before serving.

Twelve 2- to 3-ounce fillets of sole

4 tablespoons sweet butter, at room temperature

6 cups Court Bouillon (page 120) *or* Fish Stock (page 118)

Lobster Mousse

A 1½-pound live female lobster

5 cups Court Bouillon

Two 3-ounce fillets of sole

1 extra-large egg white

⅓ cup heavy cream

A pinch of salt

Sauce

3 cups Court Bouillon (retained from cooking the lobster)

¼ cup roasted bell pepper (page 88), cut into julienne strips

Salt to taste

½   cup dry white wine, preferably Muscadet or
    Sancerre

3   tablespoons heavy cream

½   pound (2 sticks) cold sweet butter, cut into
    1-inch cubes

1   teaspoon sweet Hungarian paprika

Large knife

Kitchen scissors

Cleaver

Food processor

Fine-mesh sieve

Preparing the Mousse

Among the major flavors in this dish are those of the tomalley (liver) and roe of the female lobster, which are to be found in the central cavity between the head and tail. There are two methods of killing a lobster. For the faint-hearted, the quickest way is to insert a sharp knife into the back of the head, then, holding the lobster with one hand and a sturdy large knife in the other, sever the tail from the main section of the body. However, the surest method of capturing all the flavorful juices is to hold the live lobster over a small bowl and twist the tail from the body. Reserve the juices. Whichever method you use, crack open the body with your hands or a knife and, using a small spoon, remove the green tomalley and the roe and reserve them with the juices. It is important to get the lobster to the pot quickly in order to keep the flesh from becoming mealy and deteriorating after poaching. If your fishmonger is around the corner and you are still squeamish, have him kill the lobster and collect the tomalley and roe for you.

In a 4-quart pot, bring the court bouillon to a boil, add the lobster, lower the heat, and simmer for 7–8 minutes, just long enough to firm the flesh. (The lobster will be cooked again after the mousse is wrapped in sole.) Remove the lobster and reserve the court bouillon for the sauce. Plunge the lobster into a bowl of ice water to stop the cooking process. Drain. Remove the meat from the claws and tail, using a pair of kitchen scissors and a cleaver for cracking the claws. Chop the lobster meat finely and set aside in a medium-size bowl.

Purée the sole in the food processor with the egg white and press through a fine-mesh sieve into the bowl of lobster meat. Then press the tomalley and roe through the sieve into the bowl. Add the cream and salt and blend well. If there is not a lot of juice in the lobster, you may need to add a little additional cream, no more than ⅛–¼ cup. Refrigerate until ready to use.

Making the Sauce

Measure out 3 cups of the court bouillon in which you poached the lobster and pour it into a 12-inch sauté pan. Bring it to a boil, add the red pepper and salt (taste carefully, the lobster may have given off enough), lower the heat to medium-low, and simmer until the liquid is reduced to ¾ cup. Add the wine and reduce to ¾ cup. Lower heat to a slow simmer, add the cream, reduce 3–5 minutes longer, then whisk in the cold butter, a few pieces at a time (see *Beurre Blanc* [page 27]). When all the butter has been incorporated, remove the pan from the heat and strain the sauce through a fine-mesh sieve into a clean saucepan. With the back of a spoon, push about 2 tablespoons of the now well-cooked red pepper into the sauce, then whisk in the paprika. Keep warm in a *bain-marie*, or, if necessary, the sauce may be reheated just before serving, but do not let it boil or it may separate.

Stuffing and Poaching the Fillets of Sole

Preheat the oven to 375°F. Lay a sole fillet on a flat working surface, skinned side up, and place a heaping tablespoon of lobster mousse on the thick end of the fillet about 1–2 inches from the end. Roll the fillet around the mousse, setting the roll upright when it is completed. The fillet should wrap 2–3 times around the mousse. Try to keep the bulk of the mousse toward the top, as it will cook more evenly if more exposed.

Place the rolls, mousse side up, into either twelve 1-cup ramekins (we use soup bowls) or a shallow baking dish just large enough to hold the rolls in a single layer. Pour the court bouillon over the rolls. Use the 4 tablespoons of butter to grease either 12 individual pieces of aluminum foil or 1 large piece and fit the foil tightly around the edges of the baking dish. Bake for 30 minutes. When done, remove the foil and lift out the rolls with a slotted spoon to drain off the poaching liquid. The mousse should be quite firm and, if the roe was deep green, the mousse will have turned a vivid orange.

To serve, place 2 rolls in the center of each heated serving plate and surround with 3–4 tablespoons of the sauce. Serve immediately.

Sweet-and-Sour Cabbage Stew with Apples and Meat Dumplings
4–6 servings

6½	cups tightly packed sliced red cabbage
1¼	cups finely chopped onions
¾	cup finely chopped carrots
½	white of leek, finely chopped
4	tablespoons sweet butter
1½	quarts White Stock (page 116)
1	quart water
½	cup brown sugar
½	cup sherry vinegar or cider vinegar
⅓	cup currants
1	tablespoon salt
1	teaspoon roasted garlic purée (page 81), or 2 cloves raw garlic, minced
½	teaspoon caraway seeds
1	green apple, unpeeled, cored, and diced

Dumplings

½ pound ground veal

½ pound ground pork

2 extra-large eggs

1 cup fresh bread crumbs, soaked in ¼ cup heavy cream

1 tablespoon minced shallot

⅓ cup finely chopped red bell pepper

1½ teaspoons salt

⅛ teaspoon freshly ground pepper

½ plus ⅛ teaspoon ground star anise

Combine all the dumpling ingredients and form into small balls, each a little less than a tablespoon. Refrigerate.

Preparing the Stew

In a medium-size kettle, over low heat, gently sauté the onions, carrots, and leek in the butter, cover, and allow them to stew for about 10 minutes. Then add half the cabbage, stirring so that all the vegetables are evenly coated with butter. Cover again and allow the vegetables to stew for another 8–10 minutes, being careful not to let them brown. Next, add all the other ingredients, except the remaining cabbage and the apple, and cook, covered, for 20 minutes. Add the remainder of the cabbage and cook until it is tender, about 10–15 minutes. Finally, add the dumplings and apple and poach until the dumplings are tender, about 5 minutes. Adjust the seasonings. Serve immediately.

Duck and Sausage Gumbo

8 servings

  4 Long Island (Peking) ducks

 16 Spicy Country Sausages (page 156), sautéed
     in ⅓ cup Clarified Butter (page 24)

  5 tablespoons unbleached flour

  7 tablespoons Clarified Butter, in all

  1 large yellow onion, finely chopped

  2 teaspoons plus a pinch of salt, in all

  1 bay leaf

  2 cups finely chopped celery

3–4 cups cold Duck Stock (page 117)

  1 cup red wine

  ¼ teaspoon cayenne pepper

     Freshly ground pepper to taste

  4 medium red bell peppers, finely chopped

  3 bunches scallions, thinly sliced (use all the
     white and a third of the green)

  1 tablespoon filé powder

  2 cups cooked wild rice

 16 fresh chives

*I*n a heavy 6-quart saucepan, over a low flame, gradually mix the flour into 5 tablespoons of the clarified butter, whisking slowly to form a *roux*. Stir the *roux* over a low flame until it is brown, taking care that it does not burn, about 10–15 minutes. Remove from the heat and set aside.

In a 10- to 12-inch skillet, heat 2 teaspoons of clarified butter over a medium-high flame, add the onion, 1 teaspoon of the salt, and the bay leaf, and sauté quickly, stirring frequently. When the onion is translucent, mix into the *roux*.

Using the same skillet and another 2 teaspoons of clarified butter, sauté the celery over a high flame with 1 teaspoon salt; do not brown. When the celery is cooked, but still firm, add it to the onion and *roux* mixture. Stir over a low flame for a few minutes, then slowly add 3 cups of the duck stock, stirring or whisking briskly. (If the duck stock is cold, it will mix well with the *roux* without forming lumps.) When stock and *roux* are well incorporated and smooth, turn the heat to medium and simmer gently, stirring from time to time. Meanwhile, in the skillet, reduce the red wine over a medium flame by half, then stir it into the simmering sauce along with the cayenne pepper.

While the gumbo sauce is simmering, trim the ducks: First remove the wings (freeze them for stock), then the legs and any excess flaps of skin and fat. Separate the thighs from the drumsticks. Remove the skin from the thigh pieces, place the thighs in the simmering gumbo sauce, and reduce the heat so that the liquid barely simmers. Continue to cook the sauce for 45 minutes from this point, adding more stock as needed to keep the sauce from thickening too much. Remove the sauce from the heat.

Preheat the oven to 500°F. With a cleaver or heavy chef's knife, chop off the bottom of the drumstick and slide the skin up toward the knee joint, exposing 1½–2 inches of the leg bone. Cut off the tendons with a sharp paring knife and cut away any excess fat, but leave the skin covering the remaining meat to protect it while roasting. Place the drumsticks and breasts in a shallow baking pan, sprinkle with salt and a grind of fresh pepper, and roast for 15 minutes. You may want to cover the exposed leg bones with aluminum foil to keep them from browning or possibly burning. Remove the drumsticks. If the skin on the breasts is not yet golden, raise the heat to 550°F. and continue to cook the breasts 5 minutes longer. The flesh will be rare. The gumbo may be cooked ahead to this point.

Twenty to 30 minutes before serving, preheat the oven to 550°F. Sauté the sausages in clarified butter, following the instructions on page 156. Slowly bring the gumbo to a simmer to reheat the duck thighs. Meanwhile, sauté the peppers and scallions separately and very briefly, using 2 teaspoons of clarified butter for each vegetable, and add them to the gumbo.

Carve the duck breasts from the carcasses, splitting each breast in half and then cutting each half into two pieces on the diagonal for an attractive presentation. You will have 16 pieces of boneless duck breast. Place them, skin side down, in two large cold frying pans, place over high heat, and cook until the meat sizzles. Lower the heat and sauté gently for a few minutes to render the fat, then place on a baking sheet together with the drumsticks and reheat briefly in the oven.

In the meantime, remove the duck thighs from the gumbo, bone them, and discard the bones. Whisking briskly, sprinkle the filé powder into the gumbo. Do not boil after the filé is added or the gumbo will become stringy. Adjust the seasoning; you may want to add more cayenne pepper or a little more duck stock if you want a thinner stock.

To serve, divide the sauce, drumsticks, and thigh meat evenly among 8 heated deep plates or large shallow bowls. On each plate, place 2 pieces of duck breast and 2 of the sausages. Add ¼ cup cooked wild rice and 2 chives to each plate. Serve immediately.

Lobster Gumbo with Seafood Sausages
6 servings

*F*ortunately, each element of this splendid dish can be prepared ahead of time, on the day you plan to serve it, and assembled later for a final reheating. First, make the seafood sausages, cover and set them aside (use the stock in which they poached as part of the amount needed for the gumbo); then cook the lobster and the gumbo. Serve with a crusty loaf of French bread and follow with a salad.

One	1½- to 2-pound live female lobster
6	Seafood Sausages for Gumbo (see *following recipe*), sliced
2	quarts Fish Stock (page 118)
¼	cup olive oil
1	cup finely chopped onion
½	cup chopped white of leek
½	cup finely chopped carrots
½	cup finely chopped green bell pepper
½	cup finely chopped red bell pepper
½	cup dry vermouth
1	teaspoon salt
	A large pinch of pepper
	A small pinch of cayenne pepper
1	bay leaf and ¼ teaspoon dried thyme or 3 sprigs fresh thyme, tied in a piece of washed cheesecloth
1	teaspoon filé powder

½ **cup fresh corn kernels, steamed for 3
minutes in ⅓ cup salted water** *(optional)*

½ **cup sliced okra, steamed for 8 minutes in ⅓
cup salted water** *(optional)*

2 **tablespoons minced Italian parsley** *or*
chopped fresh chives

Food processor or *blender*

The Lobster

Plunge the live lobster into boiling fish stock, cover, and cook for 3 minutes. Remove and cool lobster; reserve the stock. When lobster is cool enough to handle, break off the tail where it meets the body and, with a small spoon, gently scoop out and reserve the orange roe and the light green liver (tomalley) from the body. Split the tail lengthwise, crack the claws, and remove all the meat. Cut the tail meat into ¼-inch slices and the claw meat into small bite-size pieces and reserve. Break up the shells into 1- to 2-inch pieces, using a cleaver or kitchen scissors; reserve. Remove and discard the small sac in the top of the lobster's head. You are now ready to proceed.

Tomalley and Liver

Put tomalley and liver in a fine sieve and, with a rubber spatula or your fingers, push the mess through into a small bowl and reserve.

The Gumbo

In a medium-size frying pan, over low heat, place the olive oil and slowly sauté the onion, leek, carrots, and peppers for 8–10 minutes. Using a slotted spoon, remove the vegetables from the pan and reserve. Sauté the lobster shells in remaining oil until bright red, about 5 minutes, add the reserved fish stock and vermouth and simmer, uncovered, for 15 minutes. Strain through fine sieve and return liquid to stockpot, which has been rinsed out thoroughly. Add cooked vegetables, salt, pepper, cayenne, and bay leaf and thyme. Simmer for 15 minutes and remove from the heat.

Ladle 1½ cups of broth (with about ¼ of the vegetables) into the food processor or blender and purée. Slowly pour the tomalley and liver into the purée, blend well, and reserve.

Assembly

When ready to serve, very slowly bring the soup to a simmer, remove from heat and quickly whisk in the tomalley mixture, sprinkle in the filé powder, and stir. Heat thoroughly but *do not boil*, or the liquid will become stringy. The tomalley and filé powder will thicken the soup and give it the proper gumbo consistency. Stir in the corn, okra, sliced seafood sausages, and reserved lobster meat. Heat an additional 1–2 minutes, ladle into heated soup bowls, and sprinkle with the parsley or chives.

Seafood Sausages for Gumbo
6 sausages

Although we created these sausages especially for the Lobster Gumbo, they are good enough to be served on their own as a separate course, either as an appetizer or, if you double the ingredients, as a main course (see page 160 for Seafood Sausages with Spinach and Watercress). Serve with Vermouth Cream Sauce (page 61).

¼	pound shrimp, peeled and deveined
½	pound fillet of sole
2	extra-large egg whites
½	teaspoon minced shallot
1½	teaspoons chopped Italian parsley
1¼	teaspoons dry vermouth
½	teaspoon minced fresh chives
½	teaspoon salt
⅛	teaspoon freshly ground white pepper
	A pinch of freshly grated nutmeg
	A pinch of cayenne pepper
1	cup heavy cream
½	cup minced bay scallops

1 **quart Fish Stock (page 118)**

  Food processor

6 *pieces plastic wrap, cut 12 × 17 inches*

In the food processor, purée until smooth the shrimp and sole. Add the egg whites, one at a time, and continue to purée for about 30 seconds. Add the shallot, parsley, vermouth, chives, and seasonings. Process the mixture just until it is well mixed, then, with the motor still running, slowly add the heavy cream. Remove the mixture from the processor to a mixing bowl and stir in the minced scallops. Refrigerate for 30–45 minutes.

Fold each piece of plastic wrap in half lengthwise. Place one sixth of the sausage mixture in the center of each. Fold over one edge of the plastic wrap and gently roll the mixture until it forms a log shape 5 × 1½ inches. Twist, then tie the ends of the plastic wrap into a knot. Bring the stock to a simmer and carefully place the sausages in the broth. Do not allow the stock to boil. Cook the sausages for 15–20 minutes, turning them from time to time as they float to the surface. Remove them from the stock with a slotted spoon, unwrap, and gently blot them dry on a clean towel. Cover and reserve. Use the stock for part of the quantity needed for the soup.

Bouillabaisse

8 servings

Although it is impossible to duplicate the classic bouillabaisse of Marseilles because many of the Mediterranean fish are unavailable in the United States, nevertheless an extremely delicious version can be achieved on this side of the Atlantic using the basic aromatics and the varied gifts of our own seas. Purists may heave a sigh of distress at the introduction of shellfish, but while the shapes, colors, and flavors of these *fruits de mer* may alter the broth, they make a strong contribution to the stew.

Broth

2   cups thinly sliced onions

1   cup thinly sliced leeks

¾   cup olive oil

5   medium cloves garlic, smashed

3   quarts Fish Stock (page 118)

3   sprigs fresh thyme or 1 teaspoon dried thyme

     Peel of 1 large orange

2   bay leaves

½   teaspoon saffron threads

3   cups chopped tomatoes or canned plum tomatoes, drained

¾   cup diced fennel

1   teaspoon fennel seeds, lightly crushed

1   tablespoon peppercorns

     Kosher salt to taste

1   cup dry white wine

Fish (see NOTE)

16 hardshell clams

32 mussels

16 shrimp

 1 pound striped bass

 1 pound tile or anglerfish

 2 live lobsters (about 1¼ pounds each)

Rouille

1½ cups bouillabaisse broth

 ½ cup peeled chopped raw potato

4–6 cloves garlic

 1 red bell pepper, chopped

 1 whole red chili pepper (preferably fresh)

 ½ cup chopped parsley

Food processor or *blender*

Preparing the Broth

In a large stainless-steel or enameled kettle (not aluminum), sauté the onions and leeks gently in the olive oil until translucent, 8–10 minutes. Add the garlic, cook 5 minutes more, then add the stock, thyme, orange peel, bay leaves, saffron, tomatoes, fennel, fennel seeds, and peppercorns. Bring to a boil, lower the heat, and simmer briskly for 20 minutes. Strain through a medium sieve, pressing on the vegetables with the back of a large spoon to extract the flavorful broth. Taste for salt, allowing for more salt in the fish. Return the broth to the kettle, add the wine, and simmer 5 minutes more. Reserve separately 1½ cups of broth for the *rouille.*

Preparing the Fish

While the broth is simmering, scrub the clams and mussels under running water and remove the beards from the mussels. Peel and devein the shrimp. Have your fishmonger cut the fish into 3–4-ounce chunks with the bone in and the skin still attached.

Add the lobsters to the broth, cover, and simmer for 8 minutes, then remove. When the lobsters are cool enough to handle, divide each into 8 pieces, making certain to crack the claws.

The Rouille

Place all the *rouille* ingredients in a small stainless-steel or enameled saucepan, bring to a boil, reduce to a simmer, and cook until the potato is quite soft. Cool slightly, then purée in the food processor or blender. Let cool completely. If you have used a dried pepper, you might want to extract the pieces by putting the *rouille* through a sieve. Transfer to a sauceboat.

To Serve

Bring the broth to a boil. First, add the clams, cover, and maintain a simmer. After 3 minutes, add the mussels and the fish, cover, and simmer for 4 minutes. Now add the shrimp and the lobster. Remove and reserve any open mussels and clams so they will not overcook. Cover and simmer until the shrimp are opaque and the lobster is heated through, approximately 2 minutes.

Using a ladle and kitchen tongs, distribute all the fish and shellfish among heated soup bowls, ladle the broth over them, sprinkle with parsley, and serve, passing the *rouille* at the table. Accompany by warm French bread and good wine. Start with a simple salad.

NOTE: If the fish we suggest are out of season or not available in your region, or if you prefer others, use any combination of firm-fleshed fish Other possibilities are crabs, scallops, squid, snapper, monkfish, halibut, and sea bass. The only rule is that there be as great a variety of fish as possible and that it be sparkling fresh.

Sweets

CAKES

Very Rich Chocolate Cake (Inspired by Simca Beck)

One 10-inch cake serving 10–12

½   cup currants

½   cup bourbon

14   ounces semisweet chocolate

½   pound (2 sticks) sweet butter

5   extra-large eggs, separated

1   extra-large egg yolk

1⅓   cups sugar

½   cup plus 1 tablespoon unbleached flour

1⅓   cups Brazil nuts, toasted for 10 minutes in a preheated 350°F. oven and ground

Glaze

½   pound semisweet chocolate

¼   pound (1 stick) sweet butter

Chocolate Curls *(optional garnish)*

10-inch springform pan

*P*reheat the oven to 325°F. Butter and flour the springform pan. Soak the currants in the bourbon.

In the top of a double boiler, over simmering water, melt the chocolate and butter, transfer to a medium-size mixing bowl, and cool to lukewarm. Beat the egg yolks with the sugar until they are pale yellow, then stir into the melted chocolate.

Combine the flour with the ground nuts, stir into the batter, add the bourbon and currants and mix. Beat the egg whites until they form soft peaks, then gently fold them into the batter. Pour the batter into the pan and bake for 25 minutes. Allow the cake to cool at room temperature for 30–40 minutes before removing it from the pan.

While the cake is cooling, make the glaze. Melt the chocolate and the butter in the top of a double boiler. Make certain the butter and chocolate are thoroughly combined and that the cake is cool before glazing.

Place the cake on a serving plate, bottom side up. The bottom is flatter and will take the glaze more smoothly. Put pieces of wax paper under the cake to prevent the glaze from dripping on the plate. Pour the glaze over the cake and smooth it over the top and sides with a long, metal spatula. Remove and discard the wax paper. Refrigerate the cake for an hour and allow it to reach room temperature before serving. Serve with *Crème Anglaise* (see page 200) or whipped cream.

Life-span: 2 days, well covered, in the refrigerator

Chocolate Mousse Cake
One 10-inch cake serving 10–12

11 ounces semisweet chocolate

½ pound (2 sticks) sweet butter

5 extra-large eggs, separated

¼ cup *framboise* (raspberry liqueur) or other liqueur or brandy *(optional)*

⅓ cup sugar

¾ cup heavy cream

1 teaspoon vanilla

Optional Garnishes

1 cup heavy cream, whipped

Chocolate Curls (page 221)

10-inch springform pan

*P*reheat the oven to 350°F. Butter and flour the springform pan (see NOTE).

In the top of a double boiler, over simmering water, melt the chocolate with the butter. Transfer to a mixing bowl and allow to reach room temperature. Add the egg yolks and *framboise* and stir to mix. Beat the egg whites to soft peaks and, still beating, slowly add the sugar. Whisk a small portion of the whites into the chocolate mixture to lighten it, then fold in the remaining whites. Pour two thirds of the batter into the springform pan and bake for 20 minutes. In the meantime, whip the cream with the vanilla until stiff, fold it into the remaining batter, and refrigerate.

Allow the cake to cool for 15 minutes in the refrigerator or for 30 minutes at room temperature, then remove it from the pan by running a knife around the sides and inserting a long metal spatula underneath, gently prying the cake from the pan. Handle very carefully as the cake crumbles easily. Frost the cake with the chocolate mousse and refrigerate for 2 hours before serving.

Although the cake is delicious, it is plain in appearance, and we recommend decorating it with whipped cream piped through a pastry bag fitted with a star tube, and/or chocolate curls. If you plan to make the cake a day or two in advance, add the whipped cream just before serving.

Life-span: 2 days, well covered, in the refrigerator

NOTE: The batter can also be poured into four to six 3-inch tart tins with removable bottoms and baked for 15 minutes. Let the shells cool for 15 minutes, unmold, fill with chocolate mousse, and garnish as described.

Jane Stacey's
Hazelnut Praline Pound Cake
One cake serving 8–10

Praline Powder

½ cup superfine sugar or confectioners' sugar

1 tablespoon sweet butter, cut in small pieces

⅓ cup slivered almonds, toasted for 10 minutes in a preheated 350°F. oven (see NOTE)

Pound Cake

1 pound (4 sticks) sweet butter, at room temperature

1½ cups sugar

10 extra-large eggs

3 cups unbleached flour, sifted before measuring

2 teaspoons vanilla

2 cups skinned toasted ground hazelnuts (about ¾ pound, shelled; see NOTE)

¾ cup praline powder

Baking sheet

Food processor or blender

3-quart Bundt pan

The Praline Powder

Grease a baking sheet with oil. In a small saucepan, over very low heat, melt the sugar and butter and cook until the mixture turns golden brown and is caramelized, about 15–25 minutes. You may need to stir the sugar a few times to insure even cooking. Add the almonds, then pour the mixture onto the baking sheet, and allow to cool and harden. Do not refrigerate. Break the praline into pieces.

In the food processor or blender, grind the praline until it is pulverized into a powder. You will have approximately ¾ of a cup.

The Pound Cake

Preheat the oven to 350°F. Butter the Bundt pan. In a mixer, cream the butter with the sugar on high speed until it is light and fluffy. Lower speed to medium and add the eggs, beating after each addition, one at a time. Now, on low speed, gradually add the flour and the vanilla. Intermittently, stop the beater and scrape the bottom with a rubber spatula to make certain that there is no unincorporated butter left on the bowl. Do not overbeat. On low speed, mix in the hazelnuts and praline powder. Pour the batter into the Bundt pan, tap the pan on the counter to get rid of any air pockets, and bake for approximately 75–85 minutes, or until a knife or long toothpick inserted into the cake comes out clean. It may be necessary to cover the cake with aluminum foil during the final stages of baking to keep the top from burning. Allow the cake to cool, wrap it in aluminum foil, and store in the refrigerator.

Life-span: 1 week, well covered, in the refrigerator

NOTE: The almonds and hazelnuts can be toasted at the same time. Preheat the oven to 350°F. Place the almonds in a small shallow baking dish and the hazelnuts on a baking sheet and bake for 10 minutes. Allow the nuts to cool. To skin the hazelnuts, place them between dish towels and rub vigorously to remove as much of the skin as possible.

Crème Anglaise
Makes 2 cups

6   extra-large egg yolks

¾   cup sugar

2   cups milk

*P*lace the egg yolks in a mixing bowl, gradually add the sugar, and beat with an electric beater or a wire whisk until the mixture is pale yellow. Put the milk in a heavy-bottomed saucepan and heat it to the boiling point. Slowly add the hot milk to the eggs, stirring continuously. Return the entire mixture to the saucepan and continue to cook the custard, over medium-low heat, stirring constantly, until it is creamy and coats the back of a wooden spoon, about 20–25 minutes. The sauce is best when used fresh, but it will keep for 24 hours, covered with plastic wrap, in the refrigerator.

Marzipan Torte
One 8-inch cake serving 8–10

Cake

¼   pound (1 stick) sweet butter, at room
temperature

¾   cup sugar

6   ounces almond paste

3   extra-large eggs

1   tablespoon kirsch

¼   teaspoon almond extract

¼   cup unbleached flour, sifted before
     measuring

¼   cup ground blanched almonds

½   teaspoon grated lemon peel

Topping

Confectioners' sugar

1   quart strawberries or raspberries

Sugar to taste

Kirsch or *framboise* to taste

Drops of freshly squeezed lemon juice

8-inch springform pan

Food processor

*P*reheat the oven to 350°F. Butter the springform pan.

In a medium-size mixing bowl, cream the butter, sugar, and almond paste together until light and fluffy. Add the eggs, kirsch, and almond extract and beat well. Add the remaining ingredients and beat until thoroughly combined. Pour into the pan and bake for 40 minutes, or until golden brown. Let the cake cool completely on a rack.

Dust the cake with the confectioners' sugar and garnish with whole berries or a berry sauce made by puréeing the berries in the food processor for 30 seconds. Add sugar, liqueur, and lemon juice to taste and strain through a fine-mesh sieve to remove the seeds, if desired. Serve at room temperature.

Life-span: 2 days, well covered, in the refrigerator; bring to room temperature and add the topping components just before serving

Pumpkin Cheesecake
One 10-inch cake serving 10–12

Crust

¼   pound (1 stick) sweet butter, at room temperature

¼   cup sugar

1   cup unbleached flour

1   extra-large egg yolk

⅓   cup ground walnuts

¼   teaspoon ground cinnamon

A pinch of salt

10-inch springform pan

*P*reheat the oven to 350°F. Cream the butter and sugar until light and fluffy. Add the remaining ingredients and form into a ball. Flatten the ball and press the dough onto the bottom and up the sides of the pan. Bake until the crust is golden brown, approximately 15–20 minutes, and set aside. Lower the oven temperature to 250°F.

Filling

1½   pounds cream cheese, at room temperature

⅔   cup sugar

¾   cup dark molasses

1½   cups pumpkin purée (preferably fresh)

1   tablespoon vanilla

½   teaspoon ground ginger

1   tablespoon ground cinnamon

1   teaspoon freshly grated nutmeg

½   teaspoon ground cloves

½   teaspoon ground cardamom

1   extra-large egg

1   extra-large egg yolk

In an electric mixer, or by hand, beat the cream cheese with the sugar until there are no lumps. Add all the other ingredients except for the egg and egg yolk and mix well. Finally, add the egg and yolk and continue mixing until they are just incorporated. You do not want additional air whipped into the cheesecake. Pour into the crust and bake until the filling is set, approximately 80 minutes. Cool to room temperature in the pan and chill. Remove the pan to serve.

Life-span: 3 days, well covered, in the refrigerator

Trifle

*A*t our restaurant trifle has been a wonderful way of quickly recycling leftover desserts. Trifle is a very moist, puddinglike dessert, consisting of several layers of cake generously sprinkled with liqueur, then topped with layers of pastry cream, fresh or poached fruit, and whipped cream. It is best when it is allowed to sit for a while, so that the flavors have a chance to blend together. It is presented most beautifully in a glass bowl so that the various layers can be seen, but it can also be made in individual custard dishes. The final layer is always whipped cream, which must be put on at the last minute. There are infinite varieties possible, but here are three that we have used:

Trifle I

Very Rich Chocolate Cake (page 196), generously sprinkled with *framboise*

Chocolate mousse *or* whipped cream *or* Chocolate Pastry Cream (page 207)

Fresh raspberries

Trifle II

Marzipan Torte (page 200), without the topping, generously sprinkled with Madeira, Marsala, port, or kirsch

Pastry Cream (page 207)

Banana slices *or* poached pears

Trifle III

Hazelnut Praline Pound Cake (page 198), generously sprinkled with Grand Marnier or Cointreau

Pastry Cream (page 207)

Sliced oranges

PIES & TARTS

Chocolate Pecan Pie
One 11-inch pie serving 8–10

Crust

2   cups unbleached flour

1   tablespoon sugar

    A pinch of salt

14 tablespoons (1¾ sticks) cold sweet butter, cut in small pieces

¼   cup cold water

Filling

3   extra-large eggs

1   cup light corn syrup

1   cup sugar

¼   pound (1 stick) sweet butter, melted

4   ounces semisweet chocolate morsels or 4 ounces semisweet chocolate, melted

1½ cups pecans, toasted for 10 minutes in a preheated 350°F. oven

¼   cup dark rum

⅛   teaspoon salt

11-inch tart pan

*T*o prepare and prebake the crust, follow the instructions for *Pâte Brisée* (page 52). Lower the oven to 350°F.

While the crust is baking, combine all the filling ingredients in a medium-size mixing bowl. Pour the filling into the prebaked pie shell and bake for 50 minutes. Allow the pie to cool completely before serving.

Life-span: 2 days, well covered, in the refrigerator

Lemon Tart

One 11-inch tart serving 8–10

Crust

½	pound (2 sticks) sweet butter, at room temperature
½	cup sugar
2½	cups unbleached flour
1	extra-large egg
1	teaspoon salt

Topping

2	cups sugar
2½	lemons, thinly sliced, and each slice quartered
	Confectioners' sugar

Filling

3	cups milk
¾	cup sugar
⅓	cup unbleached flour
3	extra-large eggs
	Juice and finely grated rind of 3 lemons

11-inch tart pan

The Crust

*P*reheat the oven to 450°F. Cream the butter and the sugar together, then add the remaining ingredients. Mix until the ingredients are thoroughly incorporated and the dough comes together easily to form a ball. Pat the dough into a tart pan, making certain that it is only ⅛ inch thick. "Blind-bake" the crust for 15 minutes, following the instructions for *Pâte Brisée* (page 52). Remove the foil and bake the crust an additional 10 minutes. Allow the shell to cool to room temperature. Reduce the oven temperature to 350°F.

The Topping

While the crust is baking, combine the 2 cups sugar with 1 cup of water in a heavy-bottomed 2-quart saucepan over high heat. Boil for 10 minutes, lower the heat so that the mixture simmers, add the sliced lemons, and simmer for 25 minutes. Remove the lemon slices from the syrup with a fork, place them individually on wax paper, and cool. Discard the sugar syrup.

The Filling

Place the milk in the top of a double boiler and bring it just to a boil over direct heat. Combine the remaining filling ingredients, whisk them into the scalded milk, and place the pot over boiling water. Whisk the mixture continually until it is extremely thick; this may take up to 10 minutes. Do not allow the custard to get too hot or it may curdle. Pour the custard into the prebaked tart shell and bake for 15–20 minutes, or until it has set. Allow the tart to cool before decorating it with the candied lemon slices. Dust with confectioners' sugar. You may chill this tart for several hours or serve immediately.

Life-span: 6 hours, well covered, in the refrigerator

Papaya Tart
One 11-inch tart serving 8–10

*W*e have chosen papaya for this basic summer fruit tart, but other fruits can be used as long as they are at the peak of ripeness. Kiwis, strawberries, and seedless grapes are delicious and look appetizing covered with the shimmering glaze.

1   large ripe papaya, peeled, seeded, and cut into ⅛-inch slices

1   recipe crust from Chocolate Pecan Pie (page 204)

Pastry Cream (See Note)

1⅓   cups half-and-half

½   vanilla bean

4   extra-large eggs

3   tablespoons sugar

4   teaspoons unbleached flour

4   teaspoons cornstarch

1   tablespoon sweet butter

Glaze

½   cup apricot jam, in all

1   tablespoon rum

11-inch tart pan

Preheat the oven to 375°F. Prepare the crust, following the instructions on page 52. Allow the unbaked shell to rest in the refrigerator for 30 minutes, then "blind-bake" it for 20 minutes. Remove the foil and rice and bake for 10 minutes more. Let the shell cool.

In the meantime, in the top of a double boiler, over a medium-low flame, scald the half-and-half with the vanilla bean. In a small bowl beat the remaining pastry cream ingredients, except the butter, together until smooth. To temper the egg mixture and avoid curdling, gradually whisk ¼ cup of the scalded half-and-half into them, then gradually pour the heated eggs into the half-and-half and place over boiling water. Whisk the custard continually until it is extremely thick and holds its shape; this may take 10–15 minutes. Do not allow the pastry cream to get too hot, or it may curdle. Remove vanilla bean, pour the pastry cream into a mixing bowl, and whisk in the butter. Allow the pastry cream to cool.

In a heavy-bottomed saucepan, over medium heat, warm ¼ cup of the apricot jam until it is of spreading consistency. Brush the jam over the cooled tart shell, then spread on the cooled pastry cream and smooth it with a spatula. Arrange overlapping slices of papaya in a circular pattern over the pastry cream, beginning at the rim, covering the entire surface. In the saucepan, heat the remaining apricot jam with the rum until the mixture is of spreading consistency. Carefully brush the papaya slices with the glaze. Chill for 30 minutes and serve immediately for best results.

NOTE: To make chocolate pastry cream, add 2 ounces semisweet chocolate, melted and cooled, to the mixture just before whisking in the butter.

COOKIES

Chocolate Globs

About 21 cookies

6   ounces semisweet chocolate

2   ounces bitter chocolate

6   tablespoons sweet butter

2   extra-large eggs

1   tablespoon instant espresso

2   teaspoons vanilla

¾   cup sugar

⅓   cup unbleached flour

1   teaspoon baking powder

¼   teaspoon salt

1   cup walnuts

1   cup pecans

1   cup semisweet chocolate morsels

Baking sheet

Parchment paper

*P*reheat the oven to 325°F. Line the baking sheet with parchment paper. In the top of a double boiler, over simmering water, melt the semisweet and bitter chocolates and the butter, stirring to blend well. Allow the mixture to cool slightly.

Meanwhile, in an electric mixer fitted with a whip attachment, or with an electric hand mixer, mix the eggs, espresso, and vanilla on low speed. Add the sugar, mix until just thick, and set aside. In bowl mix together the flour, baking powder, and salt and set aside. With the mixer on low speed, add the chocolate to the eggs and blend, add the flour mixture and then the nuts and chocolate morsels, and mix well. Drop heaping tablespoons of the batter onto the baking sheet, leaving 1–1½ inches between each cookie, and bake for 15–20 minutes.

Life-span: 24 hours, well covered

Liz Sanchez's
Meringue Chocolate Chip Cookies
About 24 cookies

½   cup extra-large egg whites (about 3)

1¾   cups sugar

1   tablespoon vanilla

½   pound dry unsweetened coconut

¾   cup semisweet chocolate chip morsels

    Baking sheet

*P*reheat the oven to 350°F. Line the baking sheet with aluminum foil and butter the foil. Whip the egg whites until they are stiff, slowly add the sugar, and continue to whip for another 10 minutes. Fold in the remaining ingredients by hand. Place heaping tablespoons of batter on the baking sheet, leaving 1–1½ inches between each meringue, and bake for 15 minutes, or until the cookies are lightly browned and firm to the touch. Remove them from the foil to a rack after 2–3 minutes; otherwise they tend to stick.

Life-span: 24 hours, well covered

Gingersnaps with Fresh Ginger
About 28 cookies

3   tablespoons sweet butter

⅓   cup dark molasses

2   teaspoons grated fresh ginger

1   cup plus 2 tablespoons unbleached flour,
    sifted with ⅛ teaspoon baking soda and
    ½ teaspoon salt

Baking sheet

*P*reheat the oven to 325°F. Grease the baking sheet. Place the butter in a medium-size mixing bowl. In the top of a double boiler, heat the molasses to the boiling point and pour it over the butter. Add the ginger and mix well. Add the flour mixture, mix well, and refrigerate for 20 minutes. Roll 1 teaspoon of the dough into a ball, place it on the baking sheet, and flatten it with the floured bottom of a glass. Continue until you have used all the dough, laving 1–1½ inches between each cookie. Bake the gingersnaps for 7–8 minutes.

Life-span: 24 hours, well covered

Hazelnut-Prune Shortbread
About 25 pieces

Hazelnut Shortbread

½   pound (2 sticks) sweet butter, at room
    temperature

⅓   cup confectioners' sugar

2   cups unbleached flour

¼   teaspoon baking powder

⅓   cup ground toasted hazelnuts (about 2
    ounces, shelled, see NOTE, page 200)

*I*n a medium-size mixing bowl, cream the butter and sugar until fluffy. Mix the dry ingredients together and add all at once to the butter-sugar mixture. Stir only until well combined. Cover the dough and chill several hours or overnight. (This dough freezes well.)

Prune Filling

1	cup moist pitted prunes
2	tablespoons sweet butter
2	tablespoons currants
2	tablespoons raisins
1–3	tablespoons brandy *or* water
¼	cup sugar

Food processor
Baking sheet

Combine all the ingredients, except the sugar, in a small saucepan, cover, and cook over low heat, stirring occasionally to prevent sticking, for 25 minutes. Purée the mixture in the food processor with the sugar for 30–45 seconds, or until it is shiny and homogeneous.

Grease the baking sheet.

On a floured surface, roll the shortbread dough into a 15-inch square, approximately ⅛-inch thick. Using a ruler and pizza cutter, or a sharp knife, cut the dough into twenty-five 3-inch squares. Divide the filling into 12 portions, spread on 12 of the squares (set the extra square aside), and spread the filling to the edges of each square. Cover with the remaining squares and press the edges to seal. Cut the odd square in half on the diagonal, forming 2 triangles, spread one half with 1½ teaspoons of the filling, and cover with the other half. Place the filled shortbreads on the baking sheet and chill until firm, approximately 30 minutes.

Preheat the oven to 350°F.

Cut each filled square on the diagonal to form 2 triangles, separate the triangles on the baking sheet, and bake for about 10 minutes, or until the edges are golden brown. Allow to cool before removing from sheet.

Life-span: 2 days, well covered

Rugelach
24 rugelach

Filling

½   cup sugar

½   cup dark brown sugar

½   cup finely minced dates

2   tablespoons finely minced prunes

½   cup currants

½   heaping cup finely chopped walnuts

1   teaspoon ground cinnamon

¼   teaspoon ground cloves

⅛   teaspoon freshly grated nutmeg

1   teaspoon freshly grated lemon rind

1   teaspoon freshly squeezed lemon juice

*I*n a medium-size mixing bowl, mix thoroughly all the filling ingredients and set aside.

Dough

½   cup softened cream cheese

¼   pound (1 stick) softened sweet butter

2   cups unbleached flour

6   teaspoons apricot jam

1   extra-large egg beaten with 1 teaspoon water
    (for egg wash)

Sugar

Baking sheet

In an electric mixer or food processor, thoroughly blend the cream cheese and butter and gradually add the flour. Form the dough into a ball, wrap in wax paper, and refrigerate for 15 minutes.

Preheat the oven to 350°F. Lightly sugar and flour your work surface and generously grease the baking sheet. In a heavy-bottomed saucepan, gently warm the apricot jam until it is of spreading consistency.

Divide the dough into 4 pieces, form into balls, and roll each into a circle approximately 9–10 inches in diameter and ⅛-inch thick. Cut each round into 6 wedges and spread each wedge with ¼ teaspoon apricot jam. Place 1 heaping teaspoon of filling at the wide end of a wedge and, starting at that end, roll up the wedge, pinching and curving the ends of the finished rugelach to achieve a crescent shape. Brush the cookies with the egg wash, lightly sprinkle them with sugar, and place them 2 inches apart on the baking sheet. Bake for 20–30 minutes, or until they are golden brown. Transfer to cooling racks at once or they may stick to the sheet.

Life-span: 24 hours, well covered

BREADS

Fresh Apple Bread
2 loaves

¼   pound (1 stick) sweet butter, at room temperature

1   cup brown sugar

2   tablespoons dry sherry

1   tablespoon vanilla

3   extra-large eggs

1   cup raisins or currants

1   cup chopped nuts

1   cup chopped dates *or* apricots

1½   cups grated peeled apples

1½   tablespoons baking soda

2   cups unbleached flour

½   teaspoon salt

½   teaspoon ground cinnamon

½   teaspoon finely grated nutmeg

1   teaspoon ground coriander

2   *loaf pans, 8¼ × 4½ inches*

*P*reheat the oven to 350°F. Grease and flour the loaf pans. In a medium-size mixing bowl, cream the butter and sugar together, then add the sherry and vanilla. Add eggs, one at a time, beating well after each addition. Combine the dried fruit, nuts, and apple and add to egg mixture. Combine the dry ingredients and add to the batter in thirds, stirring just enough to combine thoroughly. Pour into the loaf pans and bake for 1 hour. Let the loaves cool on racks.

Life-span: 2–3 days, well covered, in the refrigerator

Irish Soda Bread

3 small loaves

2¼   cups unbleached flour

¼   cup sugar

½   teaspoon baking soda

½   teaspoon baking powder

¼   teaspoon salt

9   tablespoons cold sweet butter

2   teaspoons caraway seeds

¼   cup currants

¾   cup buttermilk

Baking sheet

*P*reheat the oven to 400°F. Grease the baking sheet. Combine the dry ingredients. Using a pastry blender or 2 knives, cut in the butter, caraway seeds, and currants. Add the buttermilk all at once and mix just long enough to combine. On a floured board, shape the dough into a ball, cut it into thirds, and shape into rounds. Bake the breads for 20 minutes.

Life-span: 1 day, well covered

MORE DESSERTS

Meringue Pineapple
8–10 servings

¼   recipe Pastry Cream (page 207)

1   ripe pineapple

4½ cups fresh fruit, including the fruit from the pineapple, cut into 1-inch cubes

½   cup shredded coconut

2   tablespoons Cointreau or other orange-flavored liqueur

Meringue Topping

1   cup extra-large egg whites (about 5–8 eggs)

A pinch of salt

½   cup sugar

Baking sheet

Electric mixer

Large pastry bag with ½-inch tube

*P*repare the pastry cream, following the instructions on page 207, and allow it to cool completely.

Cut the pineapple in half lengthwise, leaving on the green top leaves, and hollow it out, reserving the fruit. Reserve the juice for drinking. Discard the core. Combine all the fruit with the cooled pastry cream, coconut, and Cointreau. Divide this mixture between the two hollowed-out pineapple halves and place the halves on a baking sheet.

Preheat the oven to 325°F.

To prepare the meringue topping, with the mixer, beat the egg whites and salt until soft peaks form, then slowly add the sugar, and continue to beat until the meringue is very stiff; this may take 15–20 minutes. Place the meringue in the large pastry bag and seal the fruit completely by covering it with long vertical stripes of meringue. Next, form rosettes on top of the stripes, keeping them close together to simulate the look of a pineapple. Bake the pineapple halves for 15 minutes and serve immediately.

Watermelon Sorbet

8–10 servings

2¾   pounds ripe watermelon

2   tablespoons sugar syrup (see NOTE)

2   tablespoons freshly squeezed lemon juice

Food processor

*R*emove the rind and seeds from the watermelon and purée the flesh in the food processor; you should have about 4 cups purée. Stir in the sugar syrup and lemon juice. Adjust the amounts of sugar syrup and lemon juice to taste. Place the purée in a stainless-steel, Pyrex, or heavy plastic container, cover, and freeze completely, stirring two or three times during the process. Just before serving, purée the mixture again in the food processor until the texture is smooth. If you have trouble getting the frozen purée out of its container, dip the bottom of the container in hot water for a few seconds to loosen the sherbet from the sides.

NOTE: To make sugar syrup, bring to a boil and then cool ½ cup white sugar and ¼ cup water. (Sugar syrup is made from 2 parts sugar to 1 part water.)

Jane Stacey's Frozen Lemon Mousse
10–12 servings

6   extra-large eggs, separated

1   cup sugar syrup (2 cups sugar and 1 cup
water brought to boil and cooled)

Juice and grated rinds of 3 lemons

1¼ cups heavy cream, whipped

2   pints raspberries or strawberries, puréed and
forced through a fine-mesh strainer

8- to 9-inch springform pan

*B*utter the springform pan. Cut a piece of wax paper large enough to fit around the circumference of the pan, fold it in half lengthwise, and butter one side. Wrap the paper around the pan, butter side in, taping it so that 3–4 inches extend over the top of the pan to form a collar.

In a stainless-steel bowl and with an electric mixer or electric hand beater, beat the yolks until light and fluffy. Gradually add the cooled syrup and mix thoroughly. Place the bowl over a pot of water at a very low simmer and cook the mixture, stirring often, until thick. Remove from the heat and beat at high speed until cool. In another bowl, beat the egg whites to soft peaks. Add the lemon juice and rind to the yolk mixture and then fold in the whipped cream and the beaten whites. Pour the mousse into the springform pan and freeze, covered, 3–4 hours or overnight.

Unmold the mousse on a serving dish and serve immediately, accompanied by a purée of fresh berries.

Laura Bergman's Wild Rice Pudding
8–10 servings

1   cup raw wild rice

⅛   teaspoon salt

11   extra-large egg yolks

¾   cup plus 1 tablespoon sugar

5   cups heavy cream

2   teaspoons finely grated orange rind

⅛   teaspoon freshly grated nutmeg

¾   cup white raisins (see NOTE)

10-cup ceramic or Pyrex baking dish

*I*n a 2-quart saucepan bring 2½ cups water and the salt to a boil. Add the wild rice, lower the flame, and cook, covered, until all the water has evaporated, or until the rice is tender; this should happen simultaneously in approximately 1 hour. Allow the rice to cool.

Preheat the oven to 325°F. In a medium-size bowl or in an electric mixer, beat the yolks until they are well mixed, but not foamy. Gradually add the sugar, then stir in the heavy cream, rind, and nutmeg; the mixture should be smooth. Stir in the cooled wild rice and raisins, pour the mixture into the baking dish, and place in a *bain-marie*. Bake until the custard is set, or approximately 75 minutes. Let the custard cool and chill overnight. The following day, transfer the custard to a serving bowl and stir to distribute the custard and rice evenly. Serve chilled.

Life-span: 2 days, well covered, in the refrigerator

NOTE: Chopped dried prunes, chopped dried apricots, chopped dried figs, or currants may be substituted.

Chunky

36 pieces

2   pounds semisweet chocolate

1   pound bitter chocolate

½   pound (2 sticks) sweet butter

      A pinch of salt

3   cups dried fruit, finely chopped

1½   cups nuts, coarsely chopped

½   cup rum *or* brandy

      Jelly-roll pan, 18 × 12 × ¾ inches

*G*enerously oil the jelly-roll pan, line it with wax paper, and oil it again. Make certain that the wax paper extends over the edges of the pan to facilitate removing the candy.

In the top of a double boiler, over simmering water, melt the chocolates and butter. Remove from the heat, add the remaining ingredients, and stir to mix. Pour into the jelly-roll pan and chill overnight.

Bring to room temperature. Invert the pan on a cutting board and carefully peel off the wax paper. Then, with a heavy knife, cut into 36 pieces, 2 × 3 inches each.

Life-span: 7 days, well covered, in the refrigerator

Chocolate Curls
2 quarts

½   **pound bittersweet chocolate**

*M*elt the chocolate in a bowl over simmering, *not boiling,* water. The bottom of the bowl must *not* touch the water, as this ruins the texture of the chocolate. Melt slowly for best results. Stir until smooth and shiny, then pour onto a dry baking sheet and spread almost to the edges with a rubber spatula. It is important that the chocolate be ¹⁄₁₆–⅛ inch thick. If spread too thin, it will not curl; if too thick you will only be able to form sheets of chocolate, not curls. Chill thoroughly until the chocolate is hard. Remove from refrigerator and leave at room temperature. After 10 minutes, test the temperature of the chocolate by sinking your fingernail into it near the edge. If your fingernail makes a mark easily, but the chocolate is still firm, you are ready to make curls.

Place the straight edge of a metal pancake turner or spatula at a 45-degree angle to the chocolate and start about 1½ inches from the edge of the baking sheet. Move the spatula against and slightly under the chocolate; the chocolate will begin to curl as you cut into it, shaving it with the spatula. Turning the spatula in different directions will result in cone-shaped curls. Experiment. If your curls have frayed edges or begin to crack, the chocolate may be too cold. If fan-shaped curls form, the chocolate may be too warm; chill it again and continue making curls.

Life-span: 7–10 days, in a tightly covered plastic container, in the refrigerator

Cocktail Hors d'Oeuvre

Margaret Spader's Spiced Walnuts
4 cups

4   cups walnut halves

½   cup sugar

1   teaspoon hot pepper flakes

About 2 cups salad oil

Salt to taste

Ground cumin to taste

*B*ring 6 cups water to a boil in a 2-quart saucepan, add the walnuts, reheat to boiling, and cook 1–2 minutes. Drain in a colander or large sieve, rinse under hot running water, and shake colander to drain well. Turn the walnuts into a bowl, add the sugar and pepper flakes, and toss to coat the nuts. In a heavy-bottomed saucepan or electric skillet, heat the oil to 350°F. (The oil should be about 1 inch deep.) Add about half the walnuts and fry, stirring occasionally, until golden brown, about 5 minutes. Use a slotted spoon to remove the walnuts. Place in a sieve over a deep bowl so that the oil will drain off. Sprinkle lightly with salt and cumin and toss gently to keep the nuts from sticking together. Fry remaining walnuts.

Life-span: 1–2 months, tightly covered, in the refrigerator

Grapes Rolled in Chèvre and Pecans
24 grape-cheese balls

24   green seedless grapes

6   ounces *chèvre* (goat) cheese, at room temperature

2   ounces cream cheese

1   cup pecans

2   tablespoons walnut oil

*O*ver low heat, briefly sauté the pecans in the oil until they are golden brown, drain on paper towels, and chop them finely. Set aside. Mix the cheeses well until creamy. Place about 2 teaspoons of cheese in the palm of your hand, flatten it, and gently press grape down into it; the cheese should completely surround the grape. Roll the cheese ball around in your palm to make it smooth and round. Finally, roll the ball in the pecans until it is covered completely. Refrigerate for at least 30 minutes before serving.

Smoked Salmon Rillettes
Makes 2 cups

*T*his spread is quite beautiful served at room temperature in coronets or rosettes of sliced smoked salmon with a tiny dollop of salmon caviar and a sprig of dill or Italian parsley. Surround with toast points of black bread.

½   pound smoked salmon *or* smoked trout, sliced thinly

4   tablespoons soft sweet butter

6   tablespoons *Crème Fraîche* (page 27)

1½   tablespoons freshly squeezed lemon juice

1   teaspoon chopped fresh dill or parsley

⅛   teaspoon freshly ground white pepper

Blender or *food processor*

In the blender or food processor, purée the salmon until fairly smooth, about 30 seconds to 1 minute. A little at a time, add the remaining ingredients, adding the lemon juice and seasonings last; otherwise the mixture may separate. If for any reason it does, reconstitute by puréeing a small amount of salmon, about ¼ cup, then add the separated mixture slowly to it. The more oily smoked salmons require slightly more *crème fraîche* and butter for the texture to be light and fluffy. The oil in the salmon causes the mixture to be slightly glutinous.

Life-span: 2–3 days, well covered, in the refrigerator

Stuffed New Potatoes
40 pieces

20   new potatoes, washed

2   teaspoons salt

¼   cup grated Cheddar cheese

1   cup softened cream cheese

½   cup sour cream

3   tablespoons chopped fresh chives

½   teaspoon salt

¼   teaspoon freshly ground pepper

¼   cup chopped fresh chives or Italian parsley
    for garnish

Baking sheet

*I*n a large saucepan, cover the potatoes with about a gallon of water, add 2 teaspoons salt, and bring to a boil. Lower the flame to a medium simmer and cook until the potatoes are easily pierced with a fork, approximately 20 minutes. Drain and rinse under cool water for 1 minute.

Preheat the oven to 375°F. Cut the potatoes in half and scoop out the insides, leaving a ½-inch-thick shell. Cut a small portion of the rounded bottom off each potato so that the potatoes will sit upright easily. Place the halves on a greased baking sheet and bake for approximately 5–10 minutes, or until they are piping hot. In the meantime, combine the remaining ingredients, except the garnish, and add salt and pepper to taste. Fill each potato halfway with the mixture, garnish with the chopped herb, and serve immediately.

Spinach Roulade
10–15 slices

Roulade

¾   pound spinach leaves, well washed and tough stems removed

¼   pound (1 stick) sweet butter, in all

1¼   teaspoons salt, in all

½   teaspoon freshly ground pepper, in all

5   tablespoons unbleached flour

2   cups heavy cream

1   tablespoon Dijon mustard

1   teaspoon fresh thyme leaves

¼   teaspoon freshly grated nutmeg

6   extra-large eggs, separated

6   tablespoons grated Parmesan cheese, in all

3½   tablespoons soy oil

Smoked White Fish

¼   pound smoked white fish

1½   cups cream cheese

1   tablespoon finely chopped onion

Juice of ½ lemon

¼   teaspoon freshly ground pepper

Jelly-roll pan, 17 × 12 inches

Parchment paper

Food processor

The Roulade

*I*n a 12-inch frying pan, briefly sauté the spinach leaves in 3 tablespoons of butter with ¼ teaspoon each of salt and pepper until the leaves are wilted but still bright green in color. Drain in a strainer, cool, then place in a cloth napkin and squeeze out all the liquid. Chop the spinach finely and set aside.

Preheat the oven to 350°F. Melt 5 tablespoons of butter in a saucepan, whisk in the flour, a little at a time, and stirring constantly, cook the *roux* for 2–3 minutes. Gradually add the cream, mustard, and seasonings. Allow the mixture to cook for several minutes, then remove from the heat. Whisk in the egg yolks, 1 at a time, and add 4 tablespoons of the cheese and the chopped spinach. Beat the whites until they form soft peaks and hold their shape. Using a spatula, carefully fold the whites into the spinach mixture until no white streaks show.

Generously grease the jelly-roll pan with half the oil and line it with the parchment paper; grease the paper with the rest of the oil. Pour the roulade mixture into the pan, spreading it evenly with a spatula. Bake for approximately 25–30 minutes, or until the roulade has puffed and feels springy. Immediately invert the roulade onto a towel or a cloth napkin that has been sprinkled with the remaining 2 tablespoons of cheese. (The cheese prevents the roulade from sticking to the cloth.) Peel away the parchment paper carefully. Fold the edge of the towel over one of the long sides of the roulade and gently roll the roulade in the cloth. Set aside to cool.

The Filling

In the meantime prepare the filling. In the food processor, purée the smoked white fish, then gradually blend in the cream cheese, onion, lemon juice, and pepper.

Unroll the cooled roulade and, using a long metal cake spatula, spread the filling in a thin even layer over it. Reroll the roulade from the long side, making certain to roll it as tightly as possible. If you are not planning to serve the roulade immediately, rewrap it in a towel, then in plastic wrap, and refrigerate it. To serve, cut off the ends of the roulade and discard them, as they tend to be dried out. Slice the roulade into ½- to ¾-inch slices.

Life-span: 2 days, well covered, in the refrigerator

Mini Pissaladières

24 small pizzas

Double recipe *Pâte Brisée* (page 52)

½ cup Tomato Sauce (page 25)

½ cup coarsely chopped smoked or fresh
mozzarella

Suggested Garnishes

Chopped red or green bell peppers

Chopped prosciutto

Chopped fresh chives or parsley

Sliced pitted black olives

Sliced sautéed mushrooms

Baking sheet

Parchment paper

*P*reheat the oven to 350°F. Line the baking sheet with
the parchment paper. Roll out the dough approximately ⅛ inch thick, following the instructions on page 52. With a round cookie cutter, cut 3-inch circles,
place them on the sheet, and refrigerate for 20 minutes. Prick the rounds with a
fork at ¼-inch intervals and bake for 15–20 minutes, or until golden brown.
Remove the pan from the oven.

Turn up the heat to 450°F. Place approximately 1 teaspoonful of tomato
sauce on each round and an equal amount of cheese. Top each pizza with a
garnish or two and bake for 5 minutes, or until the cheese is melted. Serve
immediately.

Barquettes
Makes 14–16 pieces

Barquettes are miniature boat-shaped tart shells made in either fluted or straight-edged tart pans 1¾ × 4 inches. They can be filled with a sweet or savory filling.

½   recipe *Pâte Brisée* (page 52)

½–¾   cup filling (see Suggested Savory Fillings)

14–16   barquette molds

Baking sheet

14–16   pieces of aluminum foil, 4 × 6 inches each

Raw rice to fill the molds

If you plan to fill the barquettes with a savory filling, omit the sugar from the *pâte brisée* recipe and add a pinch more salt. Chill the dough thoroughly, then roll it out into a rectangle 16 × 18 inches, about ⅛ inch thick. With a sharp knife or a pizza cutter, cut the dough into 3- × 5-inch rectangles. Fit them loosely into the ungreased barquette molds and press the dough *firmly* into the corners and edges, working quickly to keep the dough from melting. Trim the edges flush with your fingers. Place the molds on the baking sheet and chill for 30 minutes, or longer, until the dough is hard.

Preheat the oven to 350°F. When the barquettes are chilled, fit the foil liners over the dough, pressing them into the edges and corners. Place the rice on the foil and bake for 10 minutes. Remove and discard the rice and liners and bake the shells 10–15 minutes longer, until golden brown. Remove shells from pans while still warm. If you wish to serve the barquettes hot, place them on the baking sheet, fill them, and bake for 2–3 minutes in a preheated 450°F. oven. Serve the barquettes as soon as possible after they are filled; otherwise they become soggy.

Suggested Savory Fillings

Hot

Crêpe fillings (pages 60–67)

Hot Ratatouille (page 36), finely chopped

Room Temperature

Chicken with Tarragon Mayonnaise (page 103), finely chopped

Tuna Curry Salad (page 102)

Egg Salad (page 92)

Filled Phyllo Triangles
24 triangles

4 sheets *phyllo* pastry, stacked
1 cup Clarified Butter (page 24)
  About 1 cup filling (pages 232–234)
  Pastry brush
  Knife
  Kitchen towel
  Baking sheet

Clean a large work surface, at least 24 × 18 inches, and brush it with some of the clarified butter. Place the stack of *phyllo* sheets on the butter, with the edges carefully aligned so that only the top sheet is exposed and with the short end of the stack facing you. Trim the edges if they are dried out. Gently brush the entire surface of the top sheet with butter. With a sharp knife, cut the stack lengthwise into 6 equal strips, cutting down through all the sheets. You will have 24 strips approximately 18 inches long by 2¼ inches wide. While folding the triangles, keep all the strips except the one you are working on covered with a damp kitchen towel to keep them from drying out.

Lift off the first strip and set it vertically on the buttered work surface. (Be careful to lift off only one strip; the *phyllo* leaves tend to stick together.) Place the suggested amount of filling at the bottom of the strip. To make the first triangle fold, turn the lower left corner up over the filling so that the bottom of the strip aligns with the right edge. Now fold the strip straight up along the top side of the triangle, then fold the whole triangle to the left so that it aligns with the left edge of the strip. Keep folding up and right, up and left, until the whole strip is used, and place the finished triangle on the baking sheet. When you have made 6 triangles, butter the next layer of 6 strips and proceed as before, until all the strips are used.

Preheat the oven to 500°F. Bake the triangles for 10–15 minutes, or until they are golden brown. Serve while still hot.

Spinach, Roquefort, and Watercress Phyllo Filling

1   pound spinach, well washed and tough stems removed

¼   pound watercress, washed and stemmed

½   cup Roquefort cheese, at room temperature

4   tablespoons sweet butter

2   shallots, finely minced

3   cloves garlic, finely minced

1   extra-large egg

1   tablespoon grated Parmesan cheese

½   teaspoon mustard

½   teaspoon freshly ground pepper

½   teaspoon salt

    A pinch of freshly grated nutmeg

In a large sauté pan, over medium heat, melt the butter, add the shallots and 2 cloves of the garlic, and sauté for 1–2 minutes. Add the spinach and watercress (you may have to do this in two batches) and sauté until they are just wilted and still bright green in color. Remove the pan from the heat and place the mixture in a sieve to drain and cool. When cool, squeeze the mixture dry in a cloth napkin. Chop the vegetables finely and place in a mixing bowl. Add all the remaining ingredients and mix well. Fill each *phyllo* strip with 1 tablespoon of the mixture.

Duxelles, Ham, and Swiss Cheese Phyllo Filling

Duxelles Mixture

1   pound mushrooms, finely chopped

2   tablespoons sweet butter

3   tablespoons minced shallot

3   tablespoons chopped Italian parsley

1   teaspoon salt

¼   teaspoon freshly ground pepper

Juice of ½ lemon

½   cup finely minced Black Forest ham

½   cup grated Swiss cheese

Preparing Duxelles

*I*n a medium-size saucepan, over low heat, sweat the shallots, covered, in the butter. Add the remaining *duxelles* ingredients and cook until all the liquid has been absorbed. Place the mixture in a clean cloth or napkin and squeeze out any remaining liquid.

To Fill Each Phyllo

½   teaspoon *duxelles*

1   teaspoon Black Forest ham

1   teaspoon grated Swiss cheese

Broccoli, Brie, and Pimiento Phyllo Filling

⅓   cup finely chopped blanched broccoli

¼   cup Brie, rind removed

¼   cup finely chopped pimiento

To Fill Each Phyllo

1   teaspoon broccoli

½   teaspoon Brie

½   teaspoon pimiento

Fresh Salmon Phyllo Filling

¾   pound salmon, cooked and finely chopped

2   tablespoons chopped fresh chives

2   tablespoons chopped fresh dill

¼   cup Spinach, Roquefort, and Watercress Filling (page 232, *optional*)

To Fill Each Phyllo

½   ounce salmon

¼   teaspoon chopped fresh chives

¼   teaspoon chopped fresh dill

½   teaspoon Spinach, Roquefort, and Watercress Filling

Crudités

Crudités—an assortment of fresh vegetables cut up for dipping—make a great centerpiece for any party. Many vegetables can be used: Carrots, celery, red and green peppers, asparagus, zucchini, cucumbers, fennel, radishes, sugar snap peas, mushrooms, scallions, string beans, blanched cauliflower and broccoli, halved plum tomatoes, red or yellow cherry tomatoes are some but not all. Look at everything in season at a good greengrocer's and choose for color and quality. Prepare the vegetables carefully and keep on ice until you arrange the *crudités* the last hour before the party.

All kinds of props and serving vessels can be thought up. Wood, glass, or ceramic bowls, baskets lined with brightly colored linen, large platters, or cake stands—some of these you certainly already have. For something special, the flat variety of wooden vegetable crate makes a great *crudités* container (your greengrocer regularly throws them away!). One of our more successful efforts, shown in *New York* magazine a few years ago, was a partitioned cherry-tomato box with the compartments filled with multicolored vegetables.

Here are a few seasonal fancies to consider. Our suggestions are minimal—what you need most is ingenuity. For fall, instead of the usual cornucopia, try a toy wheelbarrow or a hollowed-out pumpkin as the container and an arrangement of dried flowers and autumn leaves. For Christmas, experiment with a miniature tree decorated with vegetables skewered on poultry pins. (Regular ornament hooks put through the rings on the pins will hold them on the tree.) Put the rest of the vegetables on a large platter underneath. For summer, we like the vegetable crate. For spring, if you can get flowering branches at your florist, use them to frame a small, inverted Chinese umbrella used as the container. (It must be made of laminated paper, however. And sever the handle partway down so it won't jut out of your arrangement of vegetables.)

Choosing Wine

by

Alexis Bespaloff

When I first installed a telephone answering machine, in addition to the usual request to "leave your name and number," my announcement tape contained the following advice: "If this is an emergency, remember—it's red wine with meat, white with fish."

Matching wine and food has never been quite so easy, of course, and it has now been further complicated by the influence of *nouvelle cuisine*, as well as by the increasing number and variety of wines available today. While *nouvelle cuisine* is widely appealing to both professional and home cooks, it does present problems to those trying to choose appropriate wines. The use of fresh, flavorful ingredients; a freer use of such distinctive herbs and spices as green peppercorns, coriander, mint and ginger; the Oriental influence in the combination of meat and fish on the same plate; the use of fruits as garnish or ingredient, not only the ubiquitous kiwi, but also lime, black currants and orange peel; the different textures provided by vegetables—some undercooked, some combined into purées—are just a few of the recent innovations.

These new approaches to the preparation of food call for a reexamination of the traditional guidelines for selecting wines, just as the greater choice of wines now available encourages a more experimental attitude. For example, the classic wines of France are no longer the only appropriate choice at a formal dinner. California, in particular, is producing a tremendous variety of excellent wines. The range of selections from Italy has increased in a way that few people would have imagined ten years ago, and it is also possible now to find interesting wines from Spain, Portugal, central Europe, South America and Australia that were once unavailable, as well as from New York and many other states.

Rather than suggesting a number of specific wine and food combinations, however, which may be more inhibiting than helpful, I propose to examine the effects that food and wine have on each other. Once you perceive how taste, weight and texture interact, I think you'll find it much easier to choose a wine to accompany a particular dish and to avoid common pitfalls. (A brief guide to readily available types of wine will be found at the end of this chapter.)

To begin with, consider the tastes found in wine—sweetness, acidity and bitterness. Sweetness, which is present in a number of white wines and rosés and in a very few reds, often adds weight and body to an otherwise simple wine and enables it to stand up to some rich foods and seasoned dishes. (Cold diminishes the taste of sweetness, by the way, so chilling a wine that seems too sweet to you, such as an inexpensive white or red jug, will make it taste drier.)

Acidity gives wine a certain liveliness—just as a zest of lemon does to a drink, or a squeeze of lemon does to fish. Too much acidity, as in a wine made from unripe grapes, is disagreeable, but wines—especially whites—lacking sufficient acidity tend to taste flat and dull. It's the lively acidity present in many wines that makes them such suitable partners to most foods—the richness of the dish determines just how crisp a wine would best accompany it.

Some red wines, such as Bordeaux, Chianti, Rioja, and California Cabernet Sauvignon, have a slightly bitter or puckerish taste—similar to that of strong tea—that comes from the tannin extracted from the grape skins during fermentation and from the oak barrels in which some wines are aged. The puckerish taste of some young reds may overwhelm certain dishes, but other foods are complemented by a relatively assertive wine.

Sweetness, acidity and bitterness can each be discerned in, say, a cup of strong tea that also contains sugar and lemon, but their presence in wine is likely to be more subtle and balanced. Any dish that upsets that balance, however, diminishes the wine.

In addition to these three basic tastes, you should also be aware of a wine's body or weight. Just as there is a readily discernible difference between skim milk and cream, so there is between light, delicate wines and big, robust, mouth-filling ones. A wine's weight is one of the key factors in determining whether or not it will complement a particular dish. Some people also consider a wine's texture—some wines are light and simple, others rich and chewy—when matching it with foods whose textures are as different as beef, veal and fish.

With these elements in mind, it's much easier to understand how certain foods affect wines and to predict suitable combinations. A dish may complement a particular wine by matching it in taste, weight or texture; it may emphasize its qualities by providing a contrasting taste or texture; or it may distort its taste entirely.

A classic, if infrequently encountered, example of complementary tastes is Sauternes and *foie gras*. Here, the richness of Sauternes, a honeyed, luscious dessert wine, is matched by the rich texture of the *foie gras*. In the Sauternes district of France, however, this unique wine is often served with Roquefort cheese—the salty, tangy taste of the cheese providing a striking contrast to the rich, sweet wine and underscoring its taste. But serving a Sauternes with a chocolate mousse, cream-filled pastry or any other sweet dessert is usually a mistake, because the sweetness of the dessert diminishes the wine's sweetness. Poached fruit, such as pears or peaches, would complement the wine more successfully and, of course Sauternes, or any other sweet wine, can be served *as* the dessert, without the distraction of food.

A more obvious example of a dish that distorts the taste of wine is a salad with a vinegar-based dressing. The intense acidity of the vinegar has the effect of reducing the taste of acid in any wine served with it—that is, whatever acidity is present in the wine is suppressed on the palate by the stronger acidity in the dressing. The result of drinking wine with dishes that contain vinegar is that, rather than tasting too acid or vinegary, as is commonly supposed, most wines taste flat or flabby. The same general effect occurs if lemon juice is substituted for vinegar in a dressing, or if a dish contains such high-acid fruits as orange or grapefruit.

The simplest solution is not to drink wine with salad courses, which is why it may be unwise to serve cheese and salad on the same plate if you plan to accompany the cheese with an interesting bottle. If you do serve a dish that contains vinegar or another high-acid ingredient as a main course, then choose a white wine that is both assertive and high in acid, such as Sancerre, to compensate.

Mayonnaise, an oil-based sauce, has the opposite effect of vinegar's and will usually increase the acid taste in wine; this is more of a problem with reds, which may become disagreeably tart, than whites. Poached eggs, the basis of several brunch dishes, tend to dull and diminish the taste of any wine served with them, although most omelets are a good foil for wine—the type of wine depending on the omelet's filling.

Anything sweet, such as a fruit sauce, will make wine taste slightly bitter by comparison. Rich food, such as a cream-based dish or even a chestnut or vegetable purée, may make a light wine taste a bit thin by comparison. This means that the choice of vegetable purées, sauces and accompanying dishes must be taken into account when choosing wine. Incidentally, this also explains why serving champagne with a rich, sweet dessert usually diminishes the light, delicate wine and makes it taste thin and bitter.

The use of spices—peppercorns, for example—requires a wine with enough flavor and intensity to stand up to them. Very spicy foods, such as chilis, curries and certain Chinese dishes simply overwhelm wine, not because of their taste, but because the hot, burning sensation they provoke makes it virtually impossible to perceive more subtle tastes. Those who insist on wine rather than beer may want to try an assertive white wine, such as Sancerre or Gewürztraminer, or a slightly sweet one, such as any number of California Chenin Blancs and Rieslings, although if a dish is very spicy even those wines will seem flavorless. In that case, it's best to treat the wine as a refreshing beverage, as you would beer, and simply drink an inexpensive white jug wine served very cold—its temperature will be its most distinctive feature.

These examples suggest some of the problems to be aware of. But just as some combinations diminish or distort a wine, others improve a wine by modifying its taste. One of the most common examples is based on the effect of protein on tannin. A strong cup of tea tastes rather bitter, but when milk is added, the tea tastes softer—that's because the protein in milk combines with, and softens, the tannin in tea. Similarly, the protein in beef, chicken or cheese, for example, softens the tannin in such red wines as young Bordeaux, Chianti and California Cabernet Sauvignon. Thus, many red wines that seem a bit harsh or puckerish when tasted without food are more attractive when drunk with a meal.

Another example is that of a medium-sweet white wine that some people might not enjoy on its own, but which may be just right with a rich cream sauce, which diminishes the wine's sweetness. And while a pungent wine with a pronounced flavor may not be the best choice as an apéritif, it would be appropriate to serve with a seasoned dish, which will mute its assertiveness.

When selecting a wine, remember that the main ingredient in a dish— beef, chicken, fish—is often a less important guide to selecting an appropriate wine than the other ingredients with which it is to be prepared. A simply grilled fish, for example, calls for a dry white wine—the weight or acidity of the wine depending, in turn, on whether the fish is lean or oily. The same fish, baked with a rich cream sauce, might better be accompanied by a fuller-flavored white. And if the fish is sautéed in oil and garlic, the assertiveness of the wine is more important than its weight. Add tomatoes to the last dish, or a layer of cheese to the baked fish, and there are those who would choose a cool, light-bodied red wine.

A simple rack of lamb is an excellent foil for a mature and well-balanced red wine. If the lamb were to be served with a rich sauce, however, the wine would then have to be fuller-bodied and perhaps younger and more tannic as well. If the sauce also contained peppercorns, then the wine would have to be vigorous and intense enough to stand up to their spiciness. Veal and pasta, too, are dishes that can be prepared in dozens of ways, each of them calling for a somewhat different style of wine, from a light-bodied white to a robust red.

The combination of wine and cheese, considered an ideal match, deserves a few words. There's no doubt that a wedge of cheese and a young, vigorous red show each other off, especially as the protein in cheese will subdue some of the tannic harshness of the wine. If the wine is complex or mature, however, many cheeses are more likely to diminish the wine than to enhance it. A ripe, pungent Brie, a tangy goat cheese, a richly textured triple crème such as Explorateur, Boursin or St. André, and a strong blue cheese such as Roquefort are all, in their different ways, relatively assertive. The selection of an appropriate cheese may not be so important if the wine is uncomplicated and flavorful, but at many formal or wine-oriented dinners, the best and oldest wine is served last, with the cheese tray. Rather than overwhelm the mature, subtle and delicate wine that has the place of honor, it may be best to sacrifice a complete cheese tray and choose instead a mild cheese, such as an old Gouda, that will show off the wine rather than clash with it. If, on the other hand, you prefer to end a meal with a varied selection of cheeses, serve a vigorous, tannic red or a pungent white.

Although the food being served is usually the principal consideration when choosing wine, variables that are not directly related to taste sometimes play an important role as well. For example, white wine has become so fashionable in this country that many people are prepared to drink white with everything. In many parts of France, on the other hand, the vogue is to drink red with everything—even fish.

More relevant factors than fashion that affect which wine people choose are season and temperature. Most people would choose red wine with beef, but if the beef is cold and served outdoors on a warm summer day, a chilled white wine might seem more suitable. Just as many people switch from hot tea to iced tea during the summer, so many prefer chilled whites and rosés, or cool, light-bodied reds when it's warm—the wine's temperatures, weight and refreshing quality become more important than its complexity and subtlety of flavor.

Another important consideration when choosing wine is the occasion. You wouldn't serve a fine bottle at a picnic—even if the guests are knowledgeable enough to appreciate its quality, the wine makes demands on their attention that are inappropriate to the occasion. On the other hand, serving a nondescript jug wine at an elegant dinner party is a pity, as a more interesting choice invariably adds to the overall pleasure of the meal.

A SELECTION OF WINES
GROUPED BY TASTE

The recipes in this book focus, to a large extent, on dishes that are appropriate to informal entertaining without sacrificing anything in the way of taste or originality. Salads, quiches, pâtés, egg-based dishes and multi-ingredient sandwiches are not, for the most part, dishes that call for important or expensive bottles. Red and white jug wines—those available at a moderate price in 1.5-liter magnums—would be acceptable more often than not. Indeed, the modest cost of such wines from California, New York, France, Italy and elsewhere permits a host or hostess to put out carafes of both red and white wines, thus providing guests with a generous amount of wine without even having to determine which color is most appropriate with a particular dish or series of dishes.

As a general rule, well-made European reds and whites are likely to taste drier and display more lively acidity than their California counterparts, the best of which, in turn, may have more fruit and immediate appeal. With some modest experimenting, you can discover several jug wines that are neither flawed by off-tastes nor too sweet to drink with food. But as agreeable as these wines are, you may decide, at least occasionally, that flavorful dishes are best accompanied by distinctive wines that contribute their own personality to the match. I have, therefore, suggested some readily available red and white wines and grouped them by flavor characteristics rather than geographical origin. The categories are arbitrary, of course, but may be useful as a guide to the wines most suitable to accompany specific kinds of dishes.

One category of white wines includes those that are light-bodied and fresh, with some lively acidity, such as Muscadet from France's Loire Valley; such northern Italian varietal wines as Pinot Grigio, Pinot Bianco and Chardonnay; and other Italian whites such as Galestro from Tuscany and some examples of Verdicchio and Frascati. These wines would all complement light dishes.

Dry white wines with somewhat more flavor and body include Mâcon from southern Burgundy; the crisper Chablis from northern Burgundy; and a number of moderately priced California Chardonnays. These have the weight and personality to stand up to somewhat richer dishes. Whites that are even more assertive in flavor include Sancerre and Pouilly-Fumé from the Loire; certain dry white Bordeaux, including Graves; Alsace Riesling; and California Sauvignon Blanc (many of which are labeled Fumé Blanc). These wines have enough character to complement seasoned dishes, and Sancerre and Alsace Riesling in particular, with their almost aggressive acidity, can stand up to rich, fatty dishes.

Big, rich dry whites include such Burgundies as Meursault, Puligny-Montrachet and Chassagne-Montrachet, and many top California Chardonnays. These wines owe some of their richness and complexity to the new oak barrels in which they are aged, so that they are far different, not only in weight, but also in texture, from the first category of simple, light-bodied whites. They will enhance fleshy, firmly textured foods as well as those accompanied by cream sauces.

Gewürztraminer is a distinctive, spicy white whose pungent bouquet and flavor make it useful with dishes whose pronounced tastes may overwhelm many other whites. The bone dry examples from Alsace are more assertive than those from California, which are usually semidry and softer in taste, although no less distinct. Finally, there are a number of medium-sweet wines well worth considering, including German Rieslings from the Rhine and Moselle, whose lively acidity balances their sweetness, and many slightly sweet examples of California Chenin Blanc and Johannisberg Riesling. Sweetness gives a wine a little more weight and often enables it to complement certain rich dishes more successfully than a light, dry white.

Red wines, too, can be grouped by taste. Beaujolais of the most recent vintage is the best example of a light, fruity red with enough flavor and lively acidity to complement a number of dishes; somewhat similar wines include young Valpolicella and Barbera from Italy; and California Gamay and Gamay Beaujolais. Another category is that of medium-bodied reds with the brisk, slightly puckerish taste that comes from tannin, such as young Chianti, many Riojas, less expensive Bordeaux and such northern Italian varietals as Cabernet and Merlot. These wines have more character and grip, although less immediate fruit, than Beaujolais.

Reds that are more flavorful and defined include fine Bordeaux from the Médoc, St.-Emilion and Pomerol; California Cabernet Sauvignon and Merlot; Rhône wines such as Châteauneuf-du-Pape, Côte Rôtie and Hermitage; and from Italy, Barolo, Barbaresco and Brunello di Montalcino. These are all classic—and relatively expensive—reds that will enhance any meal. Another interesting choice is California Zinfandel, a distinctive, all-purpose red with a spicy, berry-like taste—some are rather light and fruity, others deep-colored, intense and tannic.

An important category of reds includes those that are mature and restrained in taste, rather than young and vigorous. Certain Riojas fall into this group, as do older Chianti Classicos and Barolos. The classic example is Bordeaux with, say, ten years of age. These are fine wines that can mature grace-fully for fifteen years or more, provided they have been properly stored. (One characteristic of fine, old red wines is that they are subtle, complex and bal-anced. Consequently, they should be served with simple dishes that will show them off—roast chicken, grilled beef, rack of lamb—rather than with compli-cated, richly sauced dishes that may overwhelm them.)

There are, in addition, two types of wine that make very good partners to certain kinds of dishes. One is dry fino sherry from Spain, which should be served chilled, like any dry white wine. A fino (or medium-dry Amontillado) may not be to everyone's taste and should not be served with a main course, but it has enough character to stand up to flavorful hors d'oeuvre, such as those made with mayonnaise, oil and garlic, or minced onions, that would over-whelm a delicate white.

Another wine that is often neglected is champagne. Sparkling wine is an excellent apéritif, of course, but it also stands up surprisingly well to certain dishes that diminish still, dry white wines, such as those with cream sauces or slightly fatty foods, such as pâtés, ham and certain fish. The bubbles in cham-pagne seem to cut across the texture of these foods and provide an attractive and refreshing contrast.

Party Planning

Taste develops the production,
the selection,
the preparation of everything that can nourish us.
Meditation 1 on the Senses—BRILLAT-SAVARIN

A party experience is always memorable. The reactions can range from ecstatic to a big yawn. Successful parties are hosted by calm, self-assured people who know that the situation is under control and are able to attend their own party and enjoy it. The key is to plan, and not to be overly ambitious—to plan with an affordable budget of both money time. We hope the suggestions in this chapter will help you feel relaxed and confident about creating a satisfying and hospitable experience for all concerned, including you.

SMALLER PARTIES

By this we mean any party you intend to do yourself with little or no help—nothing formal, but very nicely done, with wonderful food. Using a catering service for a small party can be expensive and rather forced. It's a guarded way of approaching the challenge and doesn't necessarily guarantee the best results.

There are many aspects to a good party, but here we're concerned with the menu. Decide on the number of people, plan the menu, and if, on looking it over carefully, you think you will need help, either get help or change the menu. Here are the steps we recommend in menu planning:

1. Priority! Plan according to seasonal availability of the best ingredients.

2. Consider the balance of color and texture, compatibility of flavors, and contrasting combinations of courses. *Read* recipes; their names alone don't tell you enough about what dishes are like.

3. Analyze the timing of the whole menu. Make notes like the ones next to our sample menus on what can be made ahead (and how far ahead—the life-span of dishes still served at their best), what can be partially done in advance, and what must be done at the last minute. A good look at this timing column will tell you right away if you can handle the menu, how to schedule your time, whether you need to revise it to make things work smoothly, and if you need help. (Don't overlook the possibility of volunteer help from a willing guest.) Simplify. Not every course has to be a production.

4. Be sure you have the right utensils of the right size. Party cooking can require larger pots and skillets than you normally use.

5. Be sure you have the appropriate serving dishes and think ahead to how you will present and garnish each dish. Beautiful garnishes do a lot to temper the fact that, as chief cook, you necessarily entertain informally.

6. Choose the wines, or explain the menu to the person who will choose them for you.

It saves time and money (even panic) if you check, before you shop, that all the important ingredients on your market list are available. Then market in stages if necessary, first for anything that can be prepared several days ahead, second for staples and nonperishables, third for produce and perishables. (You may want to make a work-ahead schedule similar to the one for the cocktail party on page 256.)

We offer eleven menus for you to study. Look at the advantages and/or difficulties of timing. Now plan some imaginary menus of your own and figure out the timing for them. Perhaps you want everything ready ahead; it can be done—revise accordingly. But if you're relaxed and informal, your guests will be also; messing in the kitchen just before dinner can be part of the evening's entertainment. Either way, remember, you must read each recipe you consider.

You've made a feasibility study! In no time, you'll find yourself planning a real party.

Spring or Summer Luncheon for Six

Hors d'Oeuvre Variés—three salads:	
Corn Salad II	*Life-span, 24 hours*
Broccoli with Garlic Mayonnaise	*Life-span, 6 hours; mayonnaise, 48 hours*
Marinated Beets	*Marinate 12 hours (life-span, 7 days).*
Shrimp Mousse with *Beurre Blanc* (double recipes)	*Refrigerate overnight; reheat 10–15 minutes before serving. Start sauce 30 minutes before serving and hold over warm water.*
Watermelon Sorbet	*Freeze overnight; blend in processor shortly before serving.*
Gingersnaps with Fresh Ginger	*Life-span, 24 hours*

Fall or Winter Luncheon
for Four or Six

Leek and Bell Pepper Soup	*Make ahead and reheat just before serving. (White Stock made ahead; life-span, 3–4 days.)*
Boudin Blanc with Carrot and Potato Pancakes	*Make sausages ahead (life-span, 3 days); cook and serve immediately. Pancakes can be held in 300°F. oven.*
Fresh Apple Bread	*Life-span, 2–3 days*

Spring or Summer Dinner Party
for Six

NOTE: Here's an example of a beautiful menu that could cause problems; look at the timing.

Sugar Snap Pea Soup with Mint	*Serve immediately. (White Stock made ahead; life-span, 3–4 days.)*
Sole Stuffed with Lobster Mousse with Red Pepper Sauce Vivarois	*Prepare ahead; bake 30 minutes and serve immediately. (Optional Fish Stock made ahead; freeze.) Prepare sauce 30 minutes before serving and hold over warm water.*
Mixed green salad with Vinaigrette	*Prepare ahead; toss just before serving.*
Papaya Tart	*Chill 30 minutes after baking and serve immediately.*

Spring or Summer Dinner Party for Six

NOTE: Here is a revised version of the preceding menu.

Cold Tomato-Orange Soup	*Make ahead and chill. (Optional White Stock made ahead; life-span, 3–4 days.)*
Sole Stuffed with Lobster Mousse with Red Pepper Sauce Vivarois	*Prepare ahead; bake 30 minutes and serve immediately. (Optional Fish Stock made ahead; freeze.) Start sauce 30 minutes before serving and hold over warm water.*
Mixed green salad with Vinaigrette	*Prepare ahead; toss just before serving.*
Lemon Tart	*Make ahead and chill. Life-span, 6 hours*

Fall or Winter Dinner Party for Eight

Endive and watercress salad garnished with toasted walnuts and Vinaigrette	*Prepare ahead; toss just before serving.*
Duck and Sausage Gumbo	*Make sausages ahead (life-span, 3 days). (Duck Stock made ahead; life-span, 3–4 days.) Prepare Gumbo ahead; finish 30 minutes before serving.*
Wild Rice Pudding	*Life-span, 2 days*

Spring or Summer Dinner Party for Six

Fennel Consommé	*Make ahead; reheat and garnish just before serving. (White Stock made ahead; life-span, 3–4 days.)*
Salmon Galantine (1 recipe) served warm with *Beurre Blanc* (1½ recipes) and asparagus tips	*Refrigerate overnight; reheat—and cook asparagus—10–15 minutes before serving. (Fish Stock made ahead; freeze.) Start sauce 30 minutes before serving and hold over warm water.*
***or* serve cold with Herb Mayonnaise and asparagus Vinaigrette**	*Life-span, 48 hours. Prepare ahead.*
Meringue Chocolate Chip Cookies served with sliced ripe melon	*Life-span, 24 hours only (prepare in the morning)*

Fall or Winter Supper Party for Eight or Sixteen

NOTE: In this menu, the recipes yield enough for eight. For a big party of up to sixteen, they can all be doubled. Be sure, however, that you have the utensils for the double quantities. Also, do not double the seasonings at first; start at less than double and add to taste. For sixteen this supper is best served as a buffet. Make only one Chocolate Mousse Cake and offer two desserts by adding something refreshing such as a good orange sherbet.

Cream of Celery Soup	*Make ahead; bring to a boil just before serving. (White Stock made ahead; life-span, 3–4 days.)*

Three salads: **Wild Mushroom Salad**	*Life-span, 2–3 hours at room temperature; toss periodically.*
Wild Rice Salad	*Life-span, 6 hours*
Tenderloin and Calf's Liver Salad	*Start 2–3 hours ahead; assemble immediately before serving.*
Chocolate Mousse Cake	*Life-span, 2 days*
Optional: **Orange sherbet**	*Buy the best; remove from freezer to refrigerator 3 hours before serving.*

Brunch Party for Four

Bloody Marys *or* **Mimosas (1 part orange juice to 2 parts champagne)**	
Hors d'Oeuvre: Smoked Salmon Rillettes with toasted black bread	*Life-span, 2–3 days (Bring to room temperature.)*
Seasonal cubed fruits and berries on skewers	*Prepare shortly before serving. (Optional: Marinate in balsamic vinegar and sugar.)*
Eggs Benedict with Pommes Anna Chips	*Poach eggs ahead; reheat ½ minute. Make Hollandaise ahead; hold over warm water. Start Pommes Anna Chips ahead; finish 10–15 minutes before serving (or finish, refrigerate overnight, and reheat 3–5 minutes in 500°F. oven). Heat ham and assemble immediately before serving.*
Hazelnut Praline Pound Cake	*Life-span, 1 week (To serve warm, wrap in aluminum foil and heat in 325°F. oven for 10–15 minutes.)*

Brunch Party for Eight

Mimosas (1 part orange juice to 2 parts champagne) *or* Kir Royale (1 scant teaspoon *cassis* syrup or liqueur per 8-ounce glass of champagne)	
French Toast (double recipe) Madeira-flavored Black Forest Ham (1 recipe; see Index)	*Have ready 30 minutes ahead. Reheat on baking sheet in 450°F. oven for 10 minutes to serve. Prepare ham while French Toast reheats.*
Meringue Pineapple	*Make Pastry Cream day before. Assemble pineapple and beat meringue 2 hours before guests arrive. Fifteen to 20 minutes before serving, pipe on meringue and bake in 350°F. oven.*

Outdoor Weekend Luncheon for Eight

White wine or champagne in an ice cooler	
Cold Cucumber-Yogurt Soup	*Prepare ahead and chill. (Optional White Stock made ahead; life-span, 3–4 days.)*
Scallops Seviche (double recipe)	*Life-span, 24 hours*
Curried Rice Salad	*Life-span, 6 hours*
Carrots with Rosemary (1½ recipes)	*Life-span, 2 days*
Hazelnut-Prune Shortbread and fresh raspberries	*Life-span, 2 days*

Sunday Picnic for Eight

NOTE: Everything except the breads, Gingersnaps, and bacon in this menu should be carried in sealed containers in coolers. If you aren't prepared for that, it's a grand picnic for your own backyard.

A cooler of iced tea with fresh mint, lemonade (homemade), and beer *or* rosé wine	
Sandwiches:	*Make sandwiches at picnic table.*
Smoked turkey, smoked beef, and cucumber on whole-wheat bread with Herb Mayonnaise	*Mayonnaise life-span, 48 hours. Life-span for sliced smoked cold cuts is no more than 36 hours; wrap in wax paper, then foil, and refrigerate.*
Egg Salad with red-leaf lettuce and bacon on black bread	*Egg Salad life-span, 48 hours. Cook and drain bacon last and pack separately, not in a cooler.*
Tortellini Vinaigrette with Ham and Vegetables	*Life-span, 6 hours*
Ripe tomatoes, whole or sliced	
Green Beans with Pears, Pine Nuts, and *Chèvre* (double recipe)	*Life-span, 6 hours*
Fruit salad with minced fresh mint leaves *or* whole fresh fruit	*Pears, peaches, and apples brown in fruit salad unless you use lemon juice. A good fruit salad does not have a life-span of more than 6 hours.*
Gingersnaps with Fresh Ginger	*Life-span, 24 hours*

LARGE PARTIES

By this we mean a party you won't do entirely yourself. Again, using a catering service can be expensive and not the best way to manage. And planning six months ahead will probably make you more nervous rather than less so. But planning is still the key. As an exercise in how to go about this, we have made a sample cocktail-party menu for about thirty people that you could prepare yourself. The help you need most is service—two people, one to tend bar and another to help with food. Professional help isn't necessary, just help.

We have made a work-ahead schedule that was inspired by an article in the June, 1982, issue of *Country Living* magazine and fitted it to our menu. The amount of detail may look awesome on paper, but the beauty of it is that you do what needs to be done only one stage at a time, from a month ahead down to the wire—two hours before the party. It's important that the food be in tiptop shape; set it out as late as you can during those last two hours. This is a model to apply to any party you plan. The mental organization will significantly reduce anxiety.

Cocktail Party for Thirty

Before we make you think your way through this, a note on the style of it: It is a food-oriented cocktail party, which works very well today because so many people now drink wine rather than hard liquor (though we also assume hard liquor at the bar). And we are talking about a real party, not drinks and canapés before rushing off to something else.

The Menu:

Crudités centerpiece with Red Pepper and Herb Mayonnaise (triple recipe)	*Mayonnaise life-span, 24 hours*

Cheese Board: 1 pound Brie 1 pound Cheddar ½ pound *chèvre* ½ pound Roquefort 2 bunches each green and red seedless grapes 2 cups each of dried fruits and shelled nuts Crunchy breads and crackers	
2 pounds (½ recipe) Calf's Liver Pâté *or*	*Life-span, 1 week*
2 pounds Pâté de Campagne with Green Peppercorns	*Recipe makes 3½ pounds. Life-span, 2 weeks; good to keep leftover.*
Cornichons and crusty French bread	
Circulating Hors d'Oeuvre: 60 *Barquettes* (2 recipes *Pâte Brisée*) made in 1¾- by 4-inch molds	*Life-span frozen, 2 months*
1 recipe Tuna Curry Salad (about 1 pound) to fill 30 *Barquettes*	*Life-span, 24 hours*
½ recipe Chicken with Tarragon Mayonnaise (about 1 pound), finely chopped to fill 30 *Barquettes*	*Life-span, 24 hours*
30 small skewers of pieces of cubed smoked beef, small Marinated Mushrooms (½ recipe), snow peas, and pieces of sweet red pepper	*Marinated Mushrooms life-span, 2 days*
Optional: *Sushi* combination from your local Japanese restaurant, 60 pieces	

NOTE: For some unique and magical transformations of vegetables to use for garnishes, we recommend two books: *Japanese Garnishes, The Ancient Art of Mukimono* by Yukido and Bob Haycock, Holt, Rinehart and Winston, New York; and *Japanese Cooking, A Simple Art* by Shizuo Tsuji, Kodansha International, Harper & Row, New York, distributors.

Work-ahead Schedule for Cocktail Party for Thirty

UP TO ONE MONTH AHEAD:

○ Plan buffet and bar spaces; linen, serving platters, baskets, bowls, trays; silverware and utensils; glassware (half again as many glasses as guests). For our menu: ○ **Basket** or **bowl** or special **centerpiece** for *Crudités*. ○ Large **wooden board** for cheeses and grapes. ○ **Platter** for *Pâté*. ○ **Baskets** and **bowls** for breads, crackers, dried fruits, nuts. ○ **Small bowls** for Shrimp Mayonnaise and *cornichons*. ○ **Five circulating trays** for *Barquettes*, smoked-beef skewers, and *sushi*.

○ Organize and purchase **bar requirements**. (See page 258.)
○ Bake 4 batches of ***Barquettes***; cool, wrap in foil, and freeze.
○ Arrange for **service person** and **bartender**.
○ Research **music** for the party. (See page 260.)
○ Research ***sushi*** availability.
○ Research **bar ice** availability.

UP TO ONE WEEK AHEAD:

○ Interview **service person**.
○ Plan garnishes that don't appear on menu and put on shopping list: **fresh parsley** for *Barquettes*, a **rose** for *Pâté* platter, **more flowers** for circulating hors d'oeuvre trays. Remember **skewers, cocktail napkins**.

○ Check **recipes** for **staples** and **nonperishables**; check **menu** for **nonperisha-bles**; shop for the whole list.
○ Shop for *Pâté* **ingredients** and bake the following day.
○ Order *sushi* to be delivered or picked up the day of the party.

TWO DAYS AHEAD:

○ **Order ice** for delivery in 2 days.
○ Check **recipes** for **produce** and **perishables**; shop for whole list, plus **grapes,** *Crudités* **vegetables,** and **cheeses.**
○ Prepare **Marinated Mushrooms.**

THE DAY BEFORE:

○ Chill **wine, sodas, tonic,** etc.
○ Buy and arrange **flowers.**
○ Check list of **bowls, platters, glasses, etc.** Should anything be washed, polished?
○ Make **Red Pepper and Herb Mayonnaise** for *Crudités.*
○ Make **Chicken with Tarragon Mayonnaise** and **Tuna Curry Salad.**
○ Thaw *Barquettes*, still wrapped, at room temperature.

THE DAY OF THE PARTY, MORNING:

○ Get up early. Organize space in refrigerator.
○ Cut **vegetables** for *Crudités* and store on ice or in ice water.
○ Assemble **smoked-beef skewers.**
○ Buy **fresh crusty breads.** (Is anything still needed for the bar?)
○ Clear bar and buffet space, ready for setting up.

THE DAY OF THE PARTY, AFTERNOON:

○ Crisp **Barquettes** in thin foil for 5–7 minutes in a preheated 375°F. oven.
○ Mince **parsley** for *Barquettes*.
○ Set up **cheese board**. Store in a cool place.
○ Set up *Pâté* **platter**. Store in refrigerator.
○ Have **service person** or **volunteer** arrive 2 hours before guests to help with final arrangements, pick up *sushi*, if necessary, **set up bar**, accept ice delivery.

TWO HOURS BEFORE THE PARTY:

○ Fill bowls and baskets with dried fruits, nuts, *cornichons*, crackers, sliced breads. (Reserve some bread unsliced so it won't dry out.) Arrange them and *Pâté* platter and cheese board on buffet.
○ Arrange *Crudités* and put on buffet.
○ Fill *Barquettes* with tuna and chicken salads; remember the parsley.
○ Arrange *Barquettes*, skewers, and flowers on 4 circulating trays. Leave in the kitchen.
○ Keep *sushi* on the last tray, covered with plastic wrap, in the refrigerator until moments before passing.
○ Put out bowl of Mayonnaise for *Crudités*.

LIQUID REFRESHMENT

Today, wine is right for every kind of party. You, and we, have the best possible advice on choosing it in the preceding chapter by Alexis Bespaloff.

For luncheon, some guests may prefer iced tea or coffee. For dinner, wine is always appropriate. Brunch is a special case: Hot breakfast drinks can be a good idea, several kinds of fruit juice, the old standby Bloody Mary, and wine, or champagne, budget permitting.

For the cocktail party, there are two basic ways to st up the bar:

1. The "all-wine" bar is a custom that is becoming firmly established. It is both economical and easy to service. *A guide to quantity:* 1 bottle of wine per 3 people at an all-wine bar is a reasonable estimate for the average light-drinking crowd during cocktails (1 bottle per 2–3 people is the average use during lunch or dinner).

2. The "full bar" no longer offers fancy mixed drinks; they are dated and increasingly unpopular, so we don't bother to plan for them. What you need is really governed by what you know your friends like, but here is what a caterer now considers a full bar:

Bottles: Scotch, bourbon, gin, vodka, dry vermouth, Campari, cassis syrup or liqueur for Kirs, white wine, and champagne, budget permitting.

Mixers: tonic, club soda, bitter lemon, fresh orange juice, Bloody Mary ingredients, freshly squeezed lime juice (optional). (Also an assortment of soft drinks.)

Condiments: wedges of fresh lemons and limes, cocktail onions, olives.

Ice: A generous estimate is 2 pounds per person, plus more for wine or champagne coolers. Chill as much wine and soda (and beer for picnics, etc.) as you can some days in advance of the party.

THE SERVICE

To be efficient and relaxed while hosting a large party, you need help. "Large" is, of course, a relative term; some people have a style and psychology that can absorb thirty guests at a clip with no problem. Others wouldn't be running such a party to their liking without at least one person to tend bar and another for the service of food. We can't outguess your personal style, but here are tips from our experience in both using and providing service help.

Finding help: Of course there are the employment agencies that specialize in party service. But there may be experienced help to be found at a reasonable cost through a neighborhood restaurant, a "temporaries" agency, or a local college. It is remarkable how many young people there are today who have turned to the business of food to earn money and are knowledgeable about it. As of the writing of this book in the spring of 1982, the fees for home-party help ranged from $8 to $15 per hour per service person. To cater a party for up to 50 people, we may schedule as many as five in help—two bartenders (at two bars) and three for service. Division of labor, whether hired or volunteer, is a good idea—tending bar and serving food are conflicting duties.

Up to one week in advance: Have the service person visit before the party to get acquainted with you, the kitchen, the menu, the timetable, and your expectations for assistance before, during, and after the party.

Possible items for service people: Arrive one or two hours before guests. ○ Set up bar. ○ Set up a coatrack. ○ Accept ice delivery. ○ Help set up buffet and hors d'oeuvre trays. ○ Man the front door. ○ Warm hot hors d'oeuvre. ○ Circulate hors d'oeuvre trays. ○ Slice breads, cheeses, and *pâtés* on buffet as needed. ○ Maintain party space by emptying ashtrays, collecting discarded plates, napkins, glasses. ○ Wash glasses and return to bar. ○ Take charge of final cleanup.

Luncheon- or dinner-party service: ○ Set the table. ○ Help set up platters or plates in the kitchen. ○ Pass serving dishes at table or serve at buffet. ○ Pour wine and refill when necessary. ○ Prepare coffee and cordial trays. ○ Clear the space where drinks were served before dinner. ○ Clear table. ○ Take charge of final cleanup.

THE MUSIC

We have learned that good musical intentions orchestrated by faulty judgment can nearly cause disaster . . .

One evening in the winter of 1982 we hosted a private party at the Soho Charcuterie for Costa-Gavras, the film director. After a celebrity première of his movie *Missing* at Lincoln Center, he and fifty guests headed for the restaurant for cocktails and dinner. The atmosphere was charged with excitement as guests began to arrive. The dining room in back was awash with candlelight and decorated with white branches and red roses in moss-covered vases. Soft pink and amber lights helped set the scene. Waiters, male and female, wore white tie and tails. A classical trio composed of flute, violin, and cello played selected Bach. A spectacular winterscape of *crudités* punctuated with skewers of pink shrimp was arranged on a linen-draped table near the bar.

The only problem was that the guests couldn't hear a thing anyone was saying. Bach, though softly rendered, drowned out the room. The violinist was not prepared to shift to a solo performance, so we stopped the music altogether.

But all was not lost. We switched to our cassette system, soft and distant, during cocktails. Once everyone was seated in the dining room, we set up our ensemble near the front entrance of the Charcuterie where they could entertain from afar. Whew! Close call. So, musical considerations . . .

1. Background music should be *background* music, whether you prefer classical, light swing, show tunes, or jazz. Control it either by turning your equipment down or having the speakers some distance away, or both.

2. Have live music only in a space that will not only accommodate the musicians but will also do so with room to spare for guests to move away from it—in a big room or one of two adjoining rooms. And one instrument—piano, harp, violin, guitar—may well be enough.

Have a good party!

James Beard, *American Cookery* (Boston: Little, Brown and Company, 1972).

_____*The James Beard Cookbook* (New York: E. P. Dutton & Co., Inc., 1961).

_____*Theory and Practice of Good Cooking* (New York: Alfred A. Knopf, 1979).

Simone Beck, Louisette Bertholle and Julia Child, *Mastering the Art of French Cooking* (New York: Alfred A. Knopf, 1965).

Marion Becker and Irma S. Rombauer, *The Joy of Cooking* (Indianapolis: The Bobbs-Merrill Company, Inc., 1931).

Paul Bocuse, *Paul Bocuse's French Cooking* (New York: Pantheon Books, 1977).

Julia Child, *From Julia Child's Kitchen* (New York: Alfred A. Knopf, 1970).

Alan Davidson and Jane Davidson, eds., *Dumas on Food* (London: Michael Joseph, 1978).

Mary Donovan, *The Thirteen Colonies Cookbook* (New York: Praeger Publishers, 1976).

A. Escoffier, *The Escoffier Cookbook* (New York: Crown Publishers, 1969).

Fannie Merritt Farmer, *The Boston Cooking School Cookbook* (Boston: Little, Brown and Company, 1943).

Michel Guérard, *Michel Guérard's Cuisine Minceur* (New York: William Morrow and Company, Inc., 1976).

Maida Heatter, *Book of Great Desserts* (New York: Alfred A. Knopf, 1979).

Tom Hoge, *Potato Cookery* (New York: Cornerstone Library, 1980).

Lilah Kan, *Introducing Chinese Casserole Cooking* (New York: Workman Publishing Company, Inc., 1978).

Perla Meyers, *The Seasonal Kitchen* (New York: Holt, Rinehart and Winston, 1973).

Prosper Montagné, *Larousse Gastronomique* (New York: Crown Publishers, Inc., 1961).

Raymond Oliver, *La Cuisine* (New York: Tudor Publishing Company, 1969).

Richard Olney, *Simple French Food* (New York: Atheneum, 1977).

Paula Peck, *The Art of Good Cooking* (New York: Galahad Books, 1961).

Henri Paul Pellaprat, *The Great Book of French Cuisine* (New York: Thomas Y. Crowell Company, 1966).

Jacques Pépin, *La Technique* (New York: Quadrangle, The New York Times Book Co., 1976).

Joan Scobey, ed., *The Michael Field Egg Cookbook* (New York: Holt, Rinehart and Winston, 1980).

Time-Life Books, ed., *Snacks and Sandwiches* (Alexandria, VA: Time-Life Books, 1980).

Jean Troisgros and Pierre Troisgros, *Cuisiniers à Roanne* (Paris: Robert Laffont, 1977).